Aftandil Erkinov

# *Praying For and Against the Tsar*

## Prayers and Sermons in Russian-Dominated Khiva and Tsarist Turkestan

# *Preface*

The Russian conquest of Central Asia certainly was a watershed in the region's history: New masters from far away had come, and come for good. And they were Christians, not Muslims. Thus, for the first time since the Mongols had converted to Islam, non-Muslims ruled over Muslims in Central Asia. For how much did the religious difference count? and for whom? Are we all too quick in presuming that this must have made the real difference instead of the new power structures and, over time, the new economic orientation towards Russian markets (which also meant the closing of other markets in Afghanistan and India)? How did Central Asians feel about their new masteers, how did they react to their colonizers, did they feel they were being colonized at all? or is this a concept we keep projecting into their minds?
The texts published here are some of the much more voluminous source materials discovered and partly made available by the *Zerrspiegel* project organized by the Institute of Oriental Studies, Martin-Luther-Universität Halle (you can find the database at (http://zerrspiegel.orientphil.uni-halle.de). In this project, researchers from Tashkent, Baku and St Petersburg worked together in order to find out about the mutual perceptions of colonizers and colonized in the Russian context.
The present paper starts from the assumption that prayers, private as well as public ones, are a good source for finding out what really mattered to people, what they really were concerned about. And indeed,

the two private prayers published as texts 1 and 2 in this booklet give some idea about the changes that occurred in Central Asian thinking, even if we cannot pretend that these two samples are in any way representative of what was going on in the yards of mosques and mazars all over the region.
The two public prayers, on the other hand, were elaborated on behalf of the colonial power and meant to enhance the authority the tsarist regime enjoyed in Muslim circles or wanted to enjoy. That there was no unanimity within the colonial administration is shown in the essay by the colonial administrator and intellectual N.P. Ostroumov which is equally published in this booklet. At the same time, Ostroumov's text is a fine example of Christian perception of Muslims.
The oriental sources were translated directly from the Chaghatay and Persian; thanks to Dr. Ildikó Bellér-Hann for helping with the Chaghatay. At some places, we have added some references to European research which we thought might be important, but this was not done systematically. Such references are found in the footnotes only and have not been entered into the bibliography. In other places, things evident to a Central Asian reader (but not so for a European audience) have been explained shortly in additional footnotes. All the additional material has been marked as *Translators' addition* or *Translators' note.*
Quotes from the Quran (in Ostroumov's text) have been taken from Bell's translation, quotations from the Bible from a standard English translation.

Jürgen Paul

# *Contents*


| | | |
|---|---|---|
| Introduction | | 1 |
| Text 1 | Lyrical *munājāt* on the conquest of Khiva | 3 |
| | Introduction | 3 |
| | Translation | 15 |
| Text 2 | Lyrical *munājāt* on the Russo-Japanese war | 31 |
| | Introduction | 31 |
| | Translation | 36 |
| Text 3 | *Khuṭba* for the Russian tsar and essay by Ostroumov | 39 |
| | Introduction | 39 |
| Text 3.1 | Essay by Ostroumov, translation | 49 |
| Text 3.2 | *Khuṭba*, first version, translation | 74 |
| Text 3.3 | *Khuṭba*, second version, translation | 75 |

Appendix

| | | |
|---|---|---|
| Text 1 | Lyrical *munājāt* on the conquest of Khiva | 77 |
| Text 2 | Lyrical *munājāt* on the Russo-Japanese war | 84 |
| Text 3.1 | Essay by Ostroumov | 86 |
| Text 3.2 | *Khuṭba*, first version | 101 |
| Text 3.3 | *Khuṭba*, second version | 102 |
| Text 3.4 | Persian text on a meeting in Tashkent | 103 |
| Basic Abbreviations | | 105 |
| Bibliography | | 106 |

# *Introduction*

Prayer is of one the basic characteristics of Muslim spiritual and social life. Two central forms need to be distinguished: The ritual worship *ṣalāt* and the individual prayer *duʿā* or *munājāt* which can be performed in private or in public. After the conquest of Central Asia by the Russians, prayers not only served in a private (personal) spiritual context but in addition, they obviously acquired a political touch.

The *munājāt* is a very special kind of prayer. More precisely, it is a request full of self-abasement addressed to God, and is most frequently used privately or even in secret. Over time the *munājāt* evolved into a very particular literary genre and could take on poetic forms (in rhymes). The praying person, by frequent repetitions of the text(s), endeavored to express his personal, social and, as has been mentioned, even political needs and problems. That way, for instance, in the khanate of Khiva which had become a vassal to imperial Russia, our anonymous author besought God in his *munājāt*, asking him to "remove the unbelievers (the Russians)" from his homeland.

The text of this poem is first published here from the unique manuscript.

At the outset of the 20th century the contents of the *munājāt* begin to change: Shortly after the outbreak of the Russo-Japanese war, we find almost no insults against the Russians any longer (in places, they have completely vanished). The *munājāt* was in some cases even transformed into a mouthpiece of the colonizers. In one of those poems, which was published in the press, the poet beseeches God, asking him to support the Russian emperor on his way to victory against his enemy – the Japanese (second text).

The texts of these two *munājāt* are published here in their original language and script, together with translations and comments.

In this booklet, we have also included some *khuṭba* (sermons traditionally praising God, the prophet and the ruler) that were meant for use during Friday prayers in Turkistan. *Khuṭba* sermons are a particular component of the congregational Friday worship, expressing praise for and loyalty to the ruler, for whose good health and long life the community prays. In a broad sense the *khuṭba* is a kind of expression for the good wishes of the ruler's loyal subjects. As will be shown in the following, the *khuṭba* developed in a very peculiar way not only as a political, but also as an ideological instrument within the colonial policy of the governor-generals of Turkistan (under direct administration of the tsarist government from 1867-1917). The tsarist administration created its own versions of the *khuṭba* in which the Russian emperor was proclaimed as legitimate ruler over Muslims. The text of these sermons are published here for the first time in the original language (Chaghatay) and original script. Together with them, we have chosen to publish an essay by the well-known local historiographer N. P. Ostroumov (1846-1930) along with some commenting notes.

I did not select these two seemingly not quite connected types of religious texts by chance. I will proceed on the assumption that they will allow a new idea of how changing political circumstances influenced mentality and convictions of a part of the native Muslim intelligentsia.

# *Text 1:*
# Lyrical *munājāt* on the conquest of Khiva by Russia (1873)[1]

## Introduction

During the past years the interest in the culture, history and spiritual life of Central Asia has increased. Quite a number of studies on the region have been published. Yet, the majority of these works was published by western researchers, but they have at least partly been translated into Russian.[2]
However, religious-spiritual poetry has largely remained untouched, and especially the *munājāt* genre which is the most widely spread literary form in this genre. *Munājāt* as a genre, yet again, offers some specific particularities within the regional context.

---

[1] The texts presented in this volume are linked to source material collected in the course of the "Zerrspiegel" project (head of the project: Prof. Jürgen Paul, Martin-Luther-University, Halle, Germany; manager: Beate Eschment; financial support: "VolkswagenStiftung"). The project is concerned with the research of the view on the Russian colonialization at the end of 19th–beginning of 20th century (see at http://zerrspiegel.orientphil.uni-halle.de). I want to express my special gratitude to the head of the project, as well as to my colleagues Bakhtiyar Babajanov, Ashirbek Muminov, Shadman Vakhidov and Boris Galendr for their valuable advice when writing the present study.

[2] Kleinmichel, 2000 (1,2); *Sufizm v Tsentral'noi Azii*, 2001; Krämer, 2002. - It would not serve the purpose of the present study to present a full list of what has been published on the subject in Western languages during the last few years. Translators' note.

*Munājāt* (Arabic: beseeching God, address, request, confession) – as a term derivates from Arabic, *"the verbal noun of the III verb nādjā 'to whisper to, to talk confidentially with someone'".*[3] Synonyms for *munājāt* in the different regional languages of Central Asia have been noted: in Uratebe (Tadjik republic) the word *guyāyish* is in use.[4] Another variant is *iltijā'*. In Sufi literature, this kind of spiritual poetry can serve as a synonym to characterize one of the steps or levels on the mystical path to God – *maqām-i munājāt.*[5]
*Munājāts* in verse sometimes are provided with titles like "*munājāt*", *"Munājāt-nāma"*[6], *"iltijā'-nāma"* (which means beseech in self-abasement, facing God).[7] *Munājāt* in Persian literature has been classified as a kind of religious panegyric called *qaṣīda-i dīnī.*[8]
In a broader sense the term *munājāt* denotes a private, sometimes secret or even mystical interaction with the Almighty.[9] It can contain, for instance, an address to God and a request by the author (or the praying individual) to pardon all his (or her) sins. In distinction to the traditional ritual Muslim worship *ṣalāt* (*namāz* in Persian and Uzbek as well as other Central Asian languages), the composition or recitation of this kind of poetry does not appear to be a religiously prescribed duty (*farḍ*). "Munājāt *- in distinction of* namāz *- is a nonobligatory prayer, said/held, at any time, in any form and in any*

---

[3] EI², VI,558.
[4] Sukhareva, 1975.
[5] Bertel's, 1965, 266.
[6] OIRUz-3, Nr. 3155, 39a-b.
[7] SVR, VII, Nr. 5168.
[8] Entsiklopedia adabioti va san"ati, 1989, 317-318.
[9] Farhangi farsij, 4368.

*language.*"[10] The *du'ā* (prayer in which people, in often ritualized forms, ask for something important to them), as well as the *munājāt* is seen as a free prayer by some scholars.[11] "Munājāt *becomes, however, a technical term of Muslim piety and mystical experience in the sense of* extempore prayer, *as opposed to the corporate addressing of the deity in the* ṣalāt *and of the* Ṣūfīs' *communion with God.*"[12]

By its origin the *munājāt* goes back to such pre-Islamic religions and beliefs as shamanism, the cult of ancestors and others. Shamanism, for example, was a widely spread profession, that included singing and chanting of the shaman (*bakhshī*) during his healing sessions and during seances designed to tell the future.[13] In fact such shaman texts and incantations were *munājāt.* It has also other origins and roots, which played an important role in its formation. One can point to the influences of manicheism and the cult devoted to Tengri.[14]

Moreover, the cult of ancestors must be mentioned among the very old worldviews and ritual systems which left lasting traces in the region. It can be related to shamanism[15], since in Central Asia and Kazakhstan the

---

[10] Bertel's, 1965, 266.

[11] Der Islam - III, 1990, 187.

[12] $EI^2$, VI, 558.

[13] Miropiev, 1888; Kustanaev, 1894, 45; Divaev, 1896, 34-35; 1898, 36; 1899; Kastan'e (i.e. Castagné), 1913, 1-10; Abramzon, 1958, 149; Malov, 1912; Muradov, 1975, 95-97. - This explication of the origins of *munājāt* and other ritual practices is Soviet state of the art. For other assessments, see Bruce Privratsky, *Muslim Turkestan*, Richmond (Surrey) 2001, and Theodore Levin, *The Hundred Thousand Fools of God*, Bloomington 1997, to name but two recent studies. - Translators' note.

[14] Bezertinov, 2000, 196-197. - See the addition above.

[15] Basilov, 1970; Snesarev, 1969; 1983.

cult of ancestors and saints was included into the ritual practices of the shamans.[16] The mentioning of saints or ancestors, of protecting spirits, of religious (mostly Sufi) authorities in *munājāt* texts obviously is a trace of the cult of ancestors. During shamanizing sessions, especially when telling the future, the shamans chanted *munājāt*. They repeatedly invoked the spiritis who were supposed to appear. Some of them were saints who were then asked for help as "mediators" (*shafī'*) in God's presence.[17] Addressing the Almighty through a mediator (who by the same token is a saint) is called *wasīla* (Arabic – means, arrangement); through the *wasīla* people normally turned to the Almighty.[18] Tombs and mausolea were erected for many of the holy ancestors and saints or else for pre-Muḥammadan prophets who also are asked for their intervention; often, the tombs were built in places where these persons had been honored or which had developed into centers of pilgrimage. This was the materialization of the spirits of exactly those ancestors. For that very reason the holy ancestors whose names can be found in *munājāts*, usually have tombs or mausolea in just the same place where that individual *munājāt* was composed.

In this way, in the first *munājāt* published here - dedicated to the conquest of Khiva by the Russians - more than twenty names of saints and protecting spirits are listed, who served as *wasīla* to gain the Almighty's ear. They are asked to help expulse the Russians from Khorezm.

---

[16] Tavasli, 1990, 287.

[17] Sukhareva, 1975, 69.

[18] Sukhareva, 1951.

*Munājāt* became islamized as a technical term linked to personal piety and even mystical experience. With the spread of Islam the *munājāt,* along with other more ancient religious traditions, thus, survived under a transformed, an islamized appearance. But even if it underwent this transformation, it nevertheless did not lose its preislamic characteristics, and it was particularly close to Sufism, in which the mystical connection to God plays a big role.[19]

Over time, *munājāt* becomes one of the religious and spiritual genres of Islamic poetry. Lots of texts are extant that were meant for Muslims addressing themselves to God in prayer.[20] The genre spread widely amongst Iranians and Turks, and was transformed later on into a particular genre of Persian and Turkish literature during the Islamic period.[21] In its written form, the tradition of the poetical *munājāt* goes back to classical Persian literature. In this context, the Sufi poet ʿAbdallāh Anṣārī (1006-1088) must be mentioned.[22] One of the first *munājāt* in Turki (Chaghatay) is the *"Munājāt"* by ʿAlī Shır Nawaʾı (1441-1501).[23] The transition of the *munājāt* to a separate literary genre was a very long process. It is interesting to note that the essential part of those *munājāt* that were used as ritual texts in some specific "half-

[19] Divaev, 1902; Sukhareva, 1975, 82; Iomud khan, 1924.

[20] *Arabskie rukopisi*, 1986, 178-179.

[21] See: description of handwritten *munājāt*: SVR, IV, Nr. Nr. 3401; 3429; 3432; 3446; 3457 and others; KFIR, 1989, Nr. Nr. 549; 556; Akimushkin, 1993, 23: III; 41:30; 43; 47:I; 48:IV, V, VIII; 51:159; OIRUz-1, Nr. Nr. 504 ; 531 ; 2758/2 ; 3405 ; 7386 and others (*Handlist*, 2000, 83-84). Hand written anthologies with *munājāts* in Persian and Turko-Chaghatay (OIRUz-3, Nr. 998; *İstanbul kitaplıkları*, 1947, Nr. 1).

[22] *Munajatnama-ji Hoja Abdallah Ansari*, 1376.

[23] Alisher Navoii, 1991.

shaman" mysteries, were mainly composed in Turk dialects. On the other hand, lyrical *munājāt,* that were rather considered a literary genre were written in Persian. Until the present, both types of *munājāt* survive among the population of Central Asia in one form or the other as a popular variety of Islam. There was no need for special conditions concerning this survival, since, after finishing formal ritual worship (*ṣalāt* or *namāz*) every Muslim normally reads some *du'ā* directly connected with his everyday private problems. In some way, this can be seen as some form of "mini"- *munājāt.*

Later, during the colonization of Central Asia and the establishment of the Turkestan governorate-general (1867-1917) the content of the *munājāt* was extended: the traditional description of private problems, in which the author asked God for help, tended to fade out of the center of attention. Instead, problems concerning life, society and even politics were addressed more largely. At the beginning of the 20th century in late Chagatay literature the *munājāt* almost functions as a peculiar political resonance for some or other of the moving and stormy events in tsarist Turkestan.[24] Thus, research on *munājāt* in tsarist Turkestan can yield original material for the study of the transformation of preislamic beliefs and the history of praying in Central Asia.

After the conquest of Khiva on May 29, 1290/1873 the khanate actually was transformed into a vassal of the Russian empire, ruled by Muḥammad Raḥīm khan II – Fīrūz (1864-1910). On August 12, 1873 a peace treaty between Russia and the khanate of Khiva was signed in Gandumkan, the summer residence of the khan. Under

[24] e.g., see: Sidkii Khondailikii, 1998, 111-112; Ash'or-i nisvon, 1914, 14; Ibrat, Siddikii Adzhzii, 1999, 164.

§1 of the treaty the khan of Khiva acknowledges himself a subordinate servant of the Russian emperor.[25] After these events the poet Shaydā'ī[26] published a poem in which he described his feelings concerning the conquest.[27] His poems can thus in a way be seen as an echo of the events that took place.

About five years after the conquest, in 1295/1878, our anonymous Uzbek *munājāt* was copied. This copy is kept at the Institute for Oriental Sciences, Academy of Sciences, Republic of Uzbekistan.[28] It contains 128 *bayts* (distichs) and a short concluding section in prose. The text of the poem was written in two columns, eleven lines each to the page, the text is provided with a red frame. The text was copied by Dāmullā Qurbān Niyāz. The poem appears second (foll. 251a –257a) in the manuscript, after the work "*Qiṣṣa-yi Mashrab*" (foll. 1a – 251a), a very widely spread hagiographical work about the

---

[25] The text of the treaty can be found in TsGARUz, Fond I-1, opis' 27, delo 7.

[26] Information about this poet is missing in all sources known to me. Two orally transmitted fragments from this poem are mentioned in the work of the orientalist Samoilovich (Samoilovich, 1909).

[27] OIRUz-3, Nr. 258 (KFIR, 1898, Nr. 998). On 27-28 September 2002 in Halle/Germany I presented a paper on "The Conquest of Khiva (1873) in the View of a Poet (Shaydā'ī)" (International Conference: "Looking at the Coloniser". Halle/Germany, 27-28 September, 2002, forthcoming 2004 in the MISK series, Ergon Verlag, Würzburg). The paper was written on the base of materials which I collected for the "Zerrspiegel" project. I want to express my special gratitude to the head of the project for the excellent conditions under which this conference was held. Further I want to thank the historian Palvanova, a specialist in the history of Khorezm, for her patience and support in correcting every detail of information about the socio-cultural circumstances prevailing during the period under study.

[28] OIRUz-1, Nr. 1017/2, 251a-257a. In the catalogue of the Oriental Institute, where normally brief information are given on the contents of the manuscripts the considered *munājāt* is not listed.

Central Asian Sufi Mashrab (1640-1711).[29] The manuscript measures 17,5x21,5 cm; factory-made paper, in notebook format (water mark "standing bear"). The handwriting is a careless, ordinary *nastaʿlīq*. Both works were copied by the same hand. Of course this copyist may have been the author of the poems at the same time, or else he copied a popular anonymous poem.

We have given the work the conventional title "Lyrical *munājāt* on the conquest of Khiva by Russians". The *munājāt*, emulating the genre *ḥikmat*, is written in the rhyming pattern "a-b-a-b" for the first stanza, and then it has "a-a-a-b" in the following stanzas. Essentially, the given form corresponds to a form of Turk popular poetry, the eleven syllable line (6+5=11). In this *munājāt* the same formula addressed to the Almighty recurs at the end of each quatrain: *"Oz qūdratīng bīlan yoq īt kāfirnī"*, which means: "(Oh, Lord/God), use Your power and sweep away from the face of earth those unbelievers (*kuffār*)".[30] The form of this poem, especially the kind of its rhymes, is comparable to the style of the poem the poet Shaydāʾī wrote in 1873, as mentioned above.

The *munājāt* in question was, obviously, composed by someone who originally came from the ordinary people (perhaps even by the copyist himself) and was not in full possession of the rules and secrets of the literary arts. The poem in its style and genre falls far below the poetical standards found in the literary milieu at court in Khiva. It is close to folk tradition: sometimes rhyming lines are mistakingly put together; rhetoric images and metaphors

---

[29] SVR, II, 1540.

[30] Such repetitions are characteristic for shaman incantations and spells used during healing sessions and fortune telling (Potapov, 1995, 174-178).

of court poetry are missing. All in all, the author's style is close to prayer texts used by healers for treatments.
When the author addresses the problems that occurred after the conquest of Khiva in his *munājāt,* he counts on the help of both the Almighty and the saints. The author does not escape reality, obviously he takes the superiority of the Russian forces for granted and thus does not see a more practical way of opposing the colonizers. Following tradition, he does not propose anything better than turning to God and the saints. In this, he uses the whole pantheon of Khorezmian saints, begging God for help by the intercession of all saints worshiped in Khiva. For the author the colonizers embody the enemy of Islam, the unbeliever(s), *kāfirūn* or *kuffār.* Therefore, it can be surmised that the present work represents a local Muslim response to the changing conditions after the fall of Khiva. At the beginning of the poem the anonymous author maintains that he composed his *munājāt* after the conquest of Khiva by the Russian forces. And probably enough, he was present there at that moment.
As is commonly known, in 1873 the Russian army occupied Khiva and, corresponding to the clauses of the peace treaty signed at Gandumkan on August 12, 1873, the Khanate of Khiva actually became a vassal of Russia. The poem, as the copyist states, was written in 1296/1878-79. It cannot be ruled out that the word "written" (*yāzilgan*)[31] could be read as well as the date of transcription. However, a few indicators cause doubts that it was composed in 1296/1878. In the first lines of the text, the author states that he wrote it after the coming of the Russians. The work obviously contains stark anti-colonial sentiments. Concerning Khivans, apart

[31] OIRUz-1, Nr. 1017/2, 257a.

from some rare exceptions, the author speaks of them with sympathy. He claims that the unbelievers caused huge losses among the people.

In the narrative sources that describe the events of the year 1878, a different outlook is evident. For instance, in the essay "Shajara-yi Khwārazmshāhī",[32] by Muḥammad Yūsuf Bayānī (1859-1923),[33] a Khivan court historian, the Russians are not subject to such harsh criticism. On the contrary, he claims that Russia, taking on a role as "protector" of the khanate of Khiva, saved the country from its enemies. One of the Turkoman tribes - the *Yamūt* (Yomut) - took part in revolts against the khan in 1873-1878. The Russians were on the side of Muḥammad-Raḥīm khan II in his battle against those Turkomans.[34] At any rate, concerning the *munājāt* under study, the author's open, pro-Muslim position certainly caused him to compose a poem expressing clear anti-Russian sentiments. He blamed the "unbelievers" for all the bad luck and misfortune in the daily life of the Muslims.

Thus, there is some evidence implying that the work could not possibly have been written in 1295/1878-79, as the source tries to suggest,[35] but rather during the subjugation of the khanate of Khiva itself or very shorty after the events. Let us briefly examine this evidence.

If we compare the information on the historical events of 1873 as they are described in "Shajara-yi Khārazmshāhī"[36] by Muḥammad Yūsuf Bayānī to the version

---

[32] OIRUz-1, Nr. 9596, copied in 1915 by the copyist Mullā Muḥammad Ya'qūb Usta Jum'a Niyāz oghlī (SVR, VII, Nr. 5031; edition: Baionii, 1994).

[33] Munirov, 2002, 52-60.

[34] Tukhtametov, 1969, 31-39.

[35] OIRUz-1, Nr. 1017/2, 257a.

[36] OIRUz-1, Nr. 9596.

transported in the poem,[37] the following common features can be detected:

| Nr. | Events | *Shajara-yi Khwārazm-shāhī* (OIRUz-1, Nr. 9596) | *Munājāt* on the Russian conquest of Khiva |
|---|---|---|---|
| 1. | Conquest of the fortress Manghīt | 453a-b | 35 |
| 2. | Conquest of Khiva and the citadel | 460a-462a | 11,13,17,19 |
| 3. | The khan's flight from Khiva | 456b-457a | 25-26,31 |
| 4. | Actions of the ruler's brother | 457a-459b | 63-64 |
| 5. | Actions of the court officials and army commanders in battle with the Russians | 446a-460a | 91-97,106-107 |

The details allow the conclusion that the *munājāt* was meant to describe the events of May 1873, the period of complete conquest of the khanate (Khiva surrendered on May 29). Even if the poem was literally fixed in 1878, the events described in it refer to a time not later than the beginning of June 1873.

In the given *munājāt* the principle of *wasīla* is widely used, and that means not only turning to the Almighty, but also to the saints: they are invoked in our *munājāt* and worshiped till the present day in the whole of Khorezm. For instance, the text names historical

[37] See text of the poem.

personalities (Khān-Muḥammad Raḥīm, Muḥammad Murād Dīwānbigi...), but also, and on the same level, central figures of Muslim spirituality who, however, had never been to Khorezm (ʿAlī), Sufi authorities (pīr Ismamūt, Sulṭān Vays, or Uvays) and protecting spirits (*īr, qirq qīz*) who either have no local roots and are very widely known throughout the Muslim world, or else, persons or beings who indeed serve as local patron saints or provide local centers of worship. Information on these and other personalities can be found in the comments going with the text of the poem.[38] The Sufi poet Pahlavān Maḥmūd is worth mentioning as one of the important saints of Khiva.

Of special interest is the author's reaction to the non-intervention of the saints when such misfortune befell his native country. He does not hide his astonishment, he just cannot understand why the "saints" do not help the Muslims. Sometimes he even asks himself whether the power of the "saints" is sufficient for averting the misfortune which has befallen Khiva (3,22).

Nevertheless, the end of the poem strikes an optimistic note - the author, full of hope, turns to ʿIbādallāh īshān - one of the leading spiritual authorities of Khiva.

In order to reflect the characteristics of the original text I have preserved the order of the lines and numbered them. In the text the colonizers are called "*ōruṣ*"- one Turkish spelling of the ethnonym "Russian". We translated this ethnonym in the form "Russian". The word "*kāfir*" (much more frequently used when the poet talks about

[38] For manuscript sources about saints and holy places in Khorezm, see OIRUz-1, Nr. 6895/9, 149b-153b; Nr. 7022/4, 288b-320b, copied in 1303/1885-86; Nr. 7700, copied in 1344/1925-26. (Manuscript, 2002, 158-159). For preliminary studies: Rakhmonov, Iusupov, 1963; Snesarev, 1983.

the colonizers) is translated in its original meaning "unbeliever".

## Translation

### Munājāt *on the conquest of Khiva*

### *In the name of God, the Compassionate*

*On the arrival of the shameless condemned Russian*

1. O my almighty Lord, whatever you preordain, I shall accept: with your power destroy the unbeliever!
2. We are your slaves, without power we are, how can I find a remedy? With your power destroy the unbeliever!
3. Aren't your powers enough, ḥaḍrat Pahlavān?[39] (The enemy) brought amazement to fortress and field.
4. The Muslims cry, our heart is burning, with your power ward off the unbelievers!

---

[39] Ḥaḍrat Pahlavān – Pahlavān Maḥmūd (1247-1326) – Pālvān atā, a poet and Sufi authority, especially honored in Khiva, patron saint and protector of that city. *Ḥaḍrat* means "lord" (literally: "presence"). He is the author of a philosophical *rubāʿī* (SVR, IX, Nr. 6114; published in: Pahlavon Mahmūd. Ruboiilar. Editor T. Zhalolov. Toshkent, 1962). After Muḥammad-Raḥīm khān II - Fīrūz's death in 1910, his son Asfandiyār khān (1910-1918) ascended the throne. Finishing his father's funerals on the third day of his rule, he visited the shrine of the famous poet Pahlavān Maḥmūd (OIRUz-3, Nr. 278, 5a). Pahlavān Maḥmūd is considered to be a sufi authority and a pir. His shrine was built in 1664, and in 1810-1835, it was rebuilt. Nowadays among *khalpa* women in Khorezm, Pahlavān Maḥmūd is homored as a *pīr* (Snesarev, 1983, 169-175; Kleinmichel, 2000 (1), 56-57). His shrine is in Khiva and is a place of pilgrimage. Popular legends about him are widespread, a selection was published in Khorezm (*Pakhlavon Makhmud*, 2001).

5. He laid firewood to each *masjid*[40], Lord, let none (of them) stay alive!
6. Before the Muslims come to harm, with your power destroy the unbeliever!
7. Our actions have become corrupted, we received our punishment, and if we don't die we will live in grief. (251b)
8. O prophet Nūḥ,[41] we praise you greatly, with your power destroy the unbeliever!
9. In grief we die day and night, Lord, quickly destroy the unbeliever!
10. Holy be your name to me, *qirq qīz*.[42] Don't make the believers cry, destroy the unbelievers!

---

[40] I.e. the enemy intends to burn down every *masjid*. It is worth mentioning that in the khanate of Khiva the *masjid* constituency was also an administrative unit (being the lowest rung in the local administration) and as such kept its influence also after the khanate had been abolished, during the People's Republic of Khorezm (1920-1924).

[41] Nūḥ is one of the prophets (Quran, 7:59-64), he corresponds to the Noah of the Bible. According to folk etymology, the roots of the name Khiva are connected with Nūḥ, who saved the living creatures from the deluge (*Ipak yuli*, 1993, 18-20). He also is the patron saint of the Central Asian carpenters and shipbuilders and is mentioned in their *risāla* (Snesarev, 1983, 39; the *risāla* texts in view here are regulations for crafts and craftsmen, Translators' addition ). According to a tradition which is referred to in the *Risāla-i Sairām*, the prophet Idrīs founded the city of Sairām. He asked its inhabitants to convert to Islam, but only a small part of them actually did convert. After that Nūḥ said a prayer and God send the deluge to earth. Nūḥ then took only Muslims with him on board the ark. The unbelievers died. After the deluge Nūḥ resuscitated the city of Sairām (OIRUz-1, Nr. 11367/2, 302a).

[42] *Qirq qīz* – fourty girls, in Persian – *childukhtarān* (*chihildukhtarān*), according to tradition they were brides, hiding beneath the earth from male glances (Snesarev, 1983, 50). Many places in Central Asia are connected with them. In ancient Khorezm there was a castle called *Qirq qīz* and different legends about it are known (*Ipak yuli*, 1993, 11, 77-79). A poem, "*Qirq qīz*" is widespread along the Amudarya and on the shores of the Aral sea (Tolstova, 1984, 188-215). In Khiva one of the

11. The unbeliever came, shooting at our fortress,[43] the Muslims wept and set their hopes in the Creator.
12. What should our *amīr*[44] do now? He went out and made peace. With your power destroy the unbeliever!
13. (The enemy) came in, breaking the Yangī qal'a gate,[45] I ask you for your help and support.
14. Holy be your name to me, Sayyid 'Alā' al-Dīn,[46] with your power destroy the unbeliever!
15. In front of the citadel[47] the enemy fighters marched, may the voice of my Creator be heard.

---

city quarters is called *Qirq qīz* (Babajanov, 2000, 160) and a holy place is named *Qirq qīz bībī* (Abdurasulov, 2000, 49).

[43] I.e. the attack of Khiva by Russian artillery.

[44] *Amīr* – Amīr tūra – Sayyid Muḥammad amīr al-umarā' - the elderly uncle of khan Muḥammad Raḥīm II. At the time of the Russian conquest of Khiva Muḥammad Raḥīm left the city. After his flight Sayyid Muḥammad commanded the defense of Khiva. At the beginning he personally led the negotiations with the general commander of the Russian army, the governor-general of the Turkestan *krai* (1867-1882) K. P. fon Kaufman (1818-1882). These negotiations finally led to the surrender of the city.

[45] Yangī qalā (literally "New Fortress") - one of the nine quarters of Khiva. A street with that name which leads to one of the city gates is also on record (Abdurasulov, 2000, 27, 31).

[46] Sayyid 'Alā' al-Dīn – one of the saints who are particularly honored in Khiva (d.1303). He was considered to be a great sheikh in Khorezm in the generations after Najm al-Dīn Kubrā (1145-1221) (Rakhmonov, Yusupov, 1963, 20). He had great influence. His shrine is situated in the sixth district of Khiva (*Firdavs al-iqbāl*, 1999,76) for the erection of which Amir Kulāl is given credit (died in 1371; on him, see Jürgen Paul, *Die soziale und politische Bedeutung der Naqšbandiyya in Mittelasien im 15. Jahrhundert*, Berlin 1991 – Translators' note) (Gulyamov, 1941, 18; OIRUz-1, Nr. 7700, 38a). It was rebuilt during the rule of Allāh qulī khān (1825-1843) in 1825 (Rtveladze, 1996, 62). In 1958 it was rebuilt once more (Rakhmonov, Yusupov, 1963, 21). Sayyid 'Alā' al-Dīn was the counselor of Pahlavān Maḥmūd. If pilgrims want to pay homage to the shrine of Pahlavān Maḥmūd they should first visit the grave of Sayyid 'Alā' al-Dīn. Nowadays on their wedding day, he bride and groom visit the shrine.

16. Holy be your name to me, oh my Pīr tūrt Shahbāz,[48] with your power destroy the unbelievers.
17. The unbeliever came and climbed to the top of Āq Shīkh,[49] taking the inner palace over as well.
18. Oh lord ʿAlī,[50] my *pīr*, come for revenge, with your power destroy the unbelievers! (252a)

---

[47] Ark – court, citadel of the ruler of Khiva.

[48] Pīr tūrt Shahbāz (Pir four falcons) – Tūrt Buzūrg (four great ones) – a group of four saints: 1.) Ḥasan qulī ʿazīzān; 2.) Qāḍī Muḥammad ʿazīzān; 3.) Jān Muḥammad ʿazīzān; 4.) Amīr ʿAlī ʿazīzān (OIRUz-1, Nr. 7700, 39b-40a; *Firdavs al-iqbāl*, 1999, 41.43, 558). In other versions the fourth saint is Asfandiyār I (1623-1643), who erected the shrines for the first three saints and prepared a grave for himself there. Their shrine is a burial-and memorial-complex, situated outside the walls of the ark, at the border of the quarter of Mayvastān, within the Qāra Aʿlam bābā cemetery. Until the revolution the shrine also served as a pilgrimage center; it was destroyed in 1939-1940. The minaret and the mosque have been preserved, though (Rakhmonov, Yusupov, 2000, 16-17). According to another version the place was built in 1885 (Babajanov, 2000, 159).

[49] Āq Shīkh - Āq Sheikh, Āqshīkh bābā, a legendary saint (Rtveladze, 1996, 60), who is connected to the fortress hill (rising 11 m above street level) (Gulyamov, 1941, 13-14) which is the highest spot in Khiva. It was intended as a watchtower. From its walls the post was able to overlook the whole oasis and into the desert at the borders of Khiva. It is also considered a holy place. According to folk tradition, Āq Sheikh's hermitage was located here (Khorezm, 1962, 47).

[50] ʿAlī - ʿAlī ibn Abī Ṭālib (killed in 661), son-in-law of the prophet Muḥammad and his cousin. In Central Asia there is a number of holy places connected with him. One of them is Shāh-i mardān, a symbolic grave for ʿAlī (Abashin, 1999) located in the southern part of the Ferghana valley. Another one is the shrine at Mazār-i Sharīf which gave its name to that city in northern Afghanistan (for that shrine see Robert McChesney, *Waqf in Central Asia. Four centuries in the history of a Muslim shrine.* Princeton 1991; Translators' addition). ʿAlī is especially honored in Khorezm: he is credited with the islamization of the Khorezmians (see: the part "*Ali in Khorezm*" in the book of Snesarev, 1983, 52-66). In a healing session 1930 in Khiva the female healer-*pārkhān* chanted a prayer or incantation (i.e. a *munājāt*). Along with other saints, she asked ʿAlī for help in the session (Potapov, 1995, 174,

19. Five or six of them climbed the tower, leaving the orthodox Muslims in bewilderment.
20. I raise my prayers to the Almighty Creator: with your power destroy the unbelievers!
21. May Ḥaḍrat Pahlavān once more get his cannons, and shoot your arrows at the unbelievers.
22. We didn't notice whether Pahlavān[51] is there or absent, with your power destroy the unbelievers!
23. Nobody shall remain without wealth, without servants, my Lord donates us property, nobody shall be poor or downtrodden.
24. Wealth shall be returned to us who were left in the lurch, don't make the believers cry, destroy the unbeliever!
25. Our lord the *khān*[52] left the fortress, our *amīr* sheds tears, he is distressed.
26. Our Lord, help Qirjān Īshān,[53] help faster and destroy the unbelievers!
27. Our lord the *khān* is dressed in worn-out clothes, he forgot about brocade and silk.
28. Lord, make his father and grandfather support him, with your power destroy the unbelievers!
29. The horse our Khan rode was a piebold. The nonbeliever came in and plundered the treasury. (252b)
30. Not one soul was left in the palace, be just, Lord, destroy the unbeliever!

---

178). - The Magtym (*makhdūm, makhḏūm*) are one of six Turkmen groups which together make up the honorable ("holy") class; they trace their origin to ʿAlī (Demidov, 1975, 169).

[51] I.e.: the spirit of the saint Pahlavān Maḥmūd did not oppose the Russian advance, nor did he defend us.

[52] Khān – the ruler of Khiva, Muḥammad Raḥīm khan II. When the Russians invaded Khiva, he fled.

[53] Qirjān Īshān – the name couldn't be identified so far.

31. Our lord the *khān* left the fortress with nothing, Lord saved the Muslims from disaster.
32. Day and night I beseech the Lord about just one thing: have mercy on the Muslims, destroy the unbelievers!
33. Re-install our ruler Raḥīm Khan on his throne, may the saints help him to good fortune!
34. May the unbeliever disappear, may his mere appearance be damned, with your power destroy the unbelievers!
35. Our land was thrown into disorder when the unbeliever appeared, they were galloping, apparently the unbelievers robbed everything (from the population of) Manghit.[54]
36. Nine hundred Muslims were martyred in the holy war: with your power destroy the enemy!
37. Have mercy on the old age[55] of our lord the *khān*, the unbelievers put their spoon into the *khān*'s food.
38. May the bird of fortune sit on his head once again, with your power destroy the unbelievers!
39. Lord Pahlavān return to your tomb, the unbeliever's glance fell on his cannon.
40. With your power ward off the unbeliever! Famous is your name, o Abdāl bābā.[56]

---

[54] Manghit – the name of a fortress near Khiva – one of the administrative centers of the khanate of Khiva. The fortress was captured on 20th May 1873 by the army of general commander N.A. Veriovkin, commanding the Orenburg corps of the Russian forces. Its defenders were smashed completely (OIRUz-1, Nr. 9596, 453a-b).

[55] I.e. the youth of the khan. In 1873 he was 29 years old.

[56] Abdāl bābā – a saint honored in Khorezm. According to local tradition his actual name is Aḥmad Zamchī, an army commander of Abū Muslim, the famous agent and commander of the early Abbasids. Aḥmad Zamchī is a legendary figure in Central Asian folklore. His shrine is located in the south of the factory "Uchkun" in Khiva.

41. With your power destroy the unbeliever! May he become the master of his land once again.
42. With your power destroy the unbeliever! (253a) May lord Pahlavān re-enter the fortress once again.
43. May he throw the unbeliever's head into the air, because the Muslims do not go (to the *masjid*) for prayer out of fear.
44. The rumor spread that the Russian had come, all the poor started crying.
45. With your power destroy the unbeliever! All the Muslims in their fear shut their doors.
46. Their tears split the *khān*'s chest, they turned to ʿAbdallāh *khān*[57].
47. With your power destroy the unbeliever! The unbeliever posted his soldiers in the streets.
48. Because of the lawlessness of the unbelievers, the population of Gurlān and Ghāziābād[58] left.
49. With your power destroy the unbeliever! Like the *shayṭān*, he brought much agony.
50. No rule remained in the bazaar, the unbeliever walks freely along the streets.
51. Owing to the unbeliever, our hearts burnt like in a fire, Lord, destroy the unbeliever!
52. Make the Muslims happy, and destroy the unbeliever, (253b) innumerable saints are buried in Khorezm.

---

Actually, Aḥmad Zamchī was buried in Merv (Rakhmonov, Yusupov, 1963, 16-17). In Khiva there is also a mosque, connected with the name Abdāl bābā: Urda-i Abdāl bābā (Babajanov, 2000, 160). In Khiva popular legends about him arre widespread. For example, one of them is called "*Kītāb-i Abdāl bābā ʿazīz*" (Kleinmichel, 2000 (2), 306-307).

[57] ʿAbdallāh khān – possibly ʿAbdallāh maḥram – one of the intimates of the khan, whose name appears in the description of the events of the conquest of Khiva in 1873 (OIRUz- 1, Nr. 9596, 451a).

[58] Gurlān and Ghāzi ābād – name for a place near Khiva.

53. The slaves' tears have become a river, give the land peace, God Almighty!
54. Our wish is such: Destroy the unbeliever yourself, may the unbeliever be destroyed, so they will not be able to talk about us.
55. Very soon he'll return to his land, then lord Azrā'īl[59] will come out to meet him.
56. With your power destroy the unbeliever! Listen, the language of the unbeliever – is Persian.[60]
57. Out of fear the poor don't beat their tambourines, the unbeliever scared the whole of Khorezm.
58. With your power destroy the unbeliever! The *īshāns*[61] don't say their sermons because of fear.
59. With your power destroy the unbeliever! He (the unbeliever) rebuked Nūr Makhdūm.[62]
60. He made us drink the wine of sorrow, Almighty Allāh, make them paralysed.
61. With your power destroy the unbeliever! Your name is Bābā Rīs,[63] you are descended from the Prophet.

---

[59] Azrā'īl – the angel of death.

[60] Unlike the khanates of Kokand and Bukhara, in the khanate of Khiva Persian was not spoken widely among the population. Apart from that, from the time of the invasion of Khiva by the Iranian ruler Nādir-shāh (1739) the Khivans considered the Persian Shiites their main enemies. Our author maintains that the unbelievers talk in the language of the enemies, and for him, the enemies speak Persian. During the 19th century the number of Shiite slaves in Khorezm rises. Turkmen tribes captured them in the Iranian territories bordering on Khorezm and brought them to Khiva. In Sunnite Khorezm Shiites were thought of as unbelievers. But very probably also the Russians interpreters are meant as well, who at first used Persian (Tajik) for communicating with Khivans also.

[61] The *īshāns* – Sufi sheikhs.

[62] Nūr Makhdūm – this name couldn't be identified so far.

[63] Bābā Rīs - Bābā Ra'īs, Buvarīs āta, a Khivan saint. His shrine and a mosque, named after him, are located in Khiva (Babajanov, 2000, 160).

62. May you be a guide for the *khān*. Men are hiding in swamps and steppes.
63. With your power destroy the unbeliever! (254a) Ātajān tūra[64] appeared with his army.
64. The Muslims looked at the patron with tears, Amīr bābā on his right.[65]
65. With your power destroy the unbeliever! Sulṭān Vays,[66] throw the unbeliever into the river.
66. May my supplication reach Allāh fast, your name is famous, o Narīm jān bābā.[67]
67. With your power destroy the unbeliever! Help is from you only, o my *pīr*, lord Pahlavān.

---

[64] Ātajān tūra – Sayyid Aḥmad, the younger brother of Muḥammad Raḥīm II. At the age of twenty he tried to take over power in Khiva and was arrested in 1288/1871-72. Released from prison, he tried together with Sayyid Muḥammad to lead the negotiations with the enemy. This took place during the siege of the capital, when Muḥammad Raḥīm II was absent. However, the commander-in-chief of the Russian army, K. P. fon Kaufman, didn't acknowledge them and demanded a meeting with the legal ruler of the khanate of Khiva (Description of the campaign of Khiva, 1898, 187; OIRUz-1, Nr. 9596, 459a).

[65] Amīr bābā – i.e. Amīr tūra - Sayyid Muḥammad (see above note 12). At that time supreme commander, Sayyid Muḥammad, was about seventy years old.

[66] Sulṭān Vays – a saint honored in Khorezm. Sulṭān Vays al-Qaranī (that is, Uwais al-Qaranī, a contemporary of the Prophet Muḥammad, translators' addition) is known as Sulṭān-bābā in Khorezm (OIRUz-1, Nr. 7700, 45a-51b). A mountain range at the mouth of the river Amudarya carries his name – Sultanuizdag (mountain Sultan Vays). His shrine is also located in that area (see the part on "Sultan Vais" in Snesarev, 1983, 80-100).

[67] Narīm jān bābā – on the right shore of the Amudarya when following the current downstream from Turtkul (autonomous Republic of Karakalpakistan) and until the Sultanuizdag mountain just mentioned, three famous shrines are to be found: ʿAbdallāh Narīm jān bābā, Shabbāz bābā, Sulṭān Vays (OIRUz-1, Nr. 7700, 43a-45b; Snesarev, 1983, 51). They were probably built in the 14th century (Guliamov, 1941, 21).

68. Fight against the unbelievers once more, let Shāh-i mardān[68] help you.
69. With your power destroy the unbeliever! The unbeliever prints portraits, he worships idols.
70. Oh Allāh, destroy the unbeliever completely! Your name is famous, oh lord Dāvud.[69]
71. With your power destroy the unbeliever! All the unbelievers gathered and entered the fortress.
72. In the steppe of Gandimkan[70] they caused upheaval, Lord who are the One Creator, have mercy on your slaves.
73. With your power destroy the unbeliever! They made a picture of (the tomb of) Pahlavān.
74. All visit it (the grave) in fear (of the enemy), (254b) it is hard for us, my Lord, be just.
75. With your power destroy the unbeliever! Lord Pahlavān didn't light his lantern.
76. Lord Pahlavān didn't look at the Muslims. Ishnār qashshāq[71] was afraid and didn't beat the tambourine.

---

[68] Shāh-i mardān (literally: "ruler of men", translators' note) is one of the epithets used for the caliph ʿAlī (see above). It is the name of one of the ten city gates in Khiva, thus named by Allāhqūlī khān (1825-1843) in 1841 (Rakhmonov, Yusupov, 1963, 9).

[69] Dāvud – one of the prophets (Quran 34:10-11).In the region of Kushkupir (district of Khorezm) a village was called Dāvud. In a suburb of Samarkand his grave is honored and a place of pilgrimage for the local population. In the region of Nurata (Navoi district, Uzbek Republic), in the village Sintab the Ej clan is living; they consider Dāvud their prophet. According to tradition this prophet is seen as the patron of all professions dealing with metal: blacksmiths and copper smiths (Snesarev, 1983, 39).

[70] Gandimkan – the summer residence of the ruler of Khiva.

[71] Ishnār qashshāq – according to oral information provided by Sh. Vakhidov this name is known in Khiva. Apparently, the most regular and in fact permanent visitors of the Pahlavān Maḥmūd shrine are thus called. According to tradition, a person called Ishnār qashshāq had been

77. With your power destroy the unbeliever! What sort of arrogance is it? The lord doesn't forgive such a thing.
78. The pīrs who once preached patience, don't forgive, with your power destroy the unbeliever!
79. He devastated our *amīr's* garden, our lord the khan's heart is full of burning wounds.
80. Can the unbeliever be the Muslim's enemy? With your power destroy the unbeliever!
81. Day and night I am tortured continuously by the thought: can the Muslim really become the unbeliever's slave?
82. Your name is famous, o Shāh-i zinda,[72] with your power destroy the unbeliever!
83. O my pīr Nān Yimas, you allowed people to pass over your grave,[73] God alone knows those who went astray.
84. Our days have become months, the moon does not know the sun, you who allowed people to pass over your grave, destroy the unbeliever.
85. The unbeliever turned on the *yamūt,*[74] (255a) accord your help, lord Dāvud.

---

living in the mentioned shrine. He was a *nadhr-khor* (a person living on alms and leftovers of the visitors of holy places and shrines).

[72] Shāh-i Zinda – an epithet of Qutham ibn Abbās, cousin of the prophet Muḥammad. His famous shrine is located at Samarkand where it is the center for a well-known Timurid necropolis.

[73] *Pīr nān yimas* (literally – "who does not eat bread", translators' note) – one of the local saints. The expression "*dat' dorogu nad soboi*", in Turki: *ūstūngdīn yūl bīrdīng* - means: the enemy walked over your remains, trampled the earth, and you let it happen.

[74] *Yamūt* – one of the Turkmen tribes. After the surrender of Khiva the commander-in-chief of the Russian army especially left behind in the desert a strong detachment under the command of major-general N. N. Golovachiov whose task it was to bring the Turkmen Yamūt under control; they had not yet submitted and had neither agreed to the

86. Be generous, oh my *pīr* Ismamūt,[75] with your power destroy the unbeliever!
87. May the unbeliever vanish, he burnt our fortress, but my Lord was with us and saved us.
88. I invoke also the *pīr* of Khiva, Qara Alam,[76] you who allowed people to pass over your grave, destroy the unbeliever!
89. May our *khān* regain his royal fortune once again, may God and his beloved Muḥammad be his helpers.
90. You - the skillful healer of all sufferings, with your power destroy the unbeliever!
91. May God keep the *qūsh bīgī*[77] in good health, and anywhere he treads, may the flowers blossom.
92. May the Lord destroy the unbeliever, my only Creator, destroy the Russian unbeliever.
93. When the *qūsh bīgī* marches, the unbelievers tremble with fear, when he comes, fear will shake the yazīdī[78].

---

capitulation nor laid down their arms. After 1873 the Russian forces helped the khan of Khiva to put the Yamut rebellion to an end.

[75] *Pīr* Ismamūt – Ismamūt āta, Ismī Maḥmūd āta – a saint honored in Tashauz (Dashauz, located in today's Republic of Turkmenistan). He is considered the patron of the irrigational system of Khorezm. His shrine is located in the south of Khorezm in the region of the town of Takhta and is very popular. Even the khans of Khiva visited him (see the chapter on *Ismamut ata* in Snesarev, 1983, 71-80). According to several traditions he was a missionary of Islam, sent to Khorezm by the caliphate in the 8th century (Rakhmonov, Yusupov, 1963, 14). Some reports say that Muḥammad Raḥīm II had come near the shrine of Ismamūt āta after his flight from Khiva in 1873 (OIRUz-1, Nr. 9596, 456b; Kodir Karim ugli. Ismamut ota. 1997, 29).

[76] Qara Alam – Qāra Aʿlām, one of the saints of Khiva. In this city there are a *masjid* and a cemetery called after him. One of the nine quarters is called Qāra Aʿlām (Abdurasulov, 2000, 41, 49, 52).

[77] *qūsh bīgī* – a courtly rank in the Khiva khanate. At the time discussed, Khudāyār (Khudāyār *qūsh bīgī*) held it (Tukhtametov, 1969, 37; OIRUz-1, Nr. 9596, 480a).

94. The poor people will thank God. Oh *īr*[79] and *pīr*, destroy the unbeliever! (255b)
95. When the *qūsh bīgī* approaches with full might, he will destroy grief and turn it into happiness.
96. The unbeliever's limbs tremble, oh my almighty God, destroy the unbeliever!
97. The *qūsh bīgī* says: "Never be afraid of anything, we will sow fear in the unbeliever's heart."
98. We shall destroy the Yazīdīs, God willing, with your might destroy the unbeliever!
99. The unbeliever turned the ancient fortress into a ruin, our *amīr* once again remembered God.
100. Lord, make power return to him fast, my Creator, destroy the Russian unbeliever!
101. A hero appeared and arrived in Hazārasp,[80] the unbeliever targeted the Muslim with his cannon.
102. The Lord saved him (the Muslim) once again. Always accompany us and destroy the unbeliever!
103. The *īrān*[81] all entered the fortress silently, for our deeds we were subjected to so many misfortunes.
104. Weeping bitterly I cried to my *pīr* Zārlīq bābā[82]: "Pray to the Lord, let him destroy the unbeliever!"

---

[78] The Yazīdīs – here in the sense of "people, splitting the rows of believers". Yazīd was the second caliph of the Umayyad dynasty (680-683). Tradition has it that on his order, imam Ḥusain, ʿAlī's son, was killed in the battle of Karbalā (680). After this incident the separation of Muslims into Shiites and Sunnites took place. The author equals the Russians with Yazīd.
[79] *Īr* – protecting spirit.
[80] Hazārasp – one of the administrative parts of the khanate of Khiva.
[81] *Īrān* – plural of *īr*.
[82] Zārlīq bābā – Munglīq-Zārlīq bābā – one of the saints honored in Turkestan. His shrine is located in the region of Chardar, at the border to Uzbekistan and Kazakhstan.

105. I will be your sacrifice, oh Ilyās and Khiḍr,[83] you are God's slave, close to him, destroy the unbeliever! (256a)
106. The *dīvan bīgī*'s name is Muḥammad Murād,[84] he didn't pay the soldiers.
107. Ya'qub bāy,[85] Maḥmūd Niyāz[86] returned to Qongrāt,[87] my Lord, destroy the Russian unbeliever!
108. The *īr* will come and help the country, we will be saved from misfortune and trust in the Almighty.
But here someone stopped our 'Ibādallah īshān[88] and told him: "The situation of the country is getting worse. You are one of the honoured. Try to prevent this." And they went on (addressing him).

109. You are the Axis of the world, the *pīr* of both worlds, be informed about the things going on around!
110. There is no doubt left in your soul, be informed about the situation in the country!

---

[83] Ilyās – one of the prophets (Quran 6:85; 37:123-130).
[84] Muḥammad Murād - Muḥammad Murād dīvān bīgī –dīvān bīgī ("prime minister") at the court of Muḥammad Raḥīm II, formerly an Afghan slave. Head of the anti-Russian party in Khiva and organizer of military action against the Russian invasion in 1873. He accompanied the khan to the capitulation ceremony and was arrested (June 2, 1873) on the order of commander-in-chief K. P. fon Kaufman. He stayed under arrest as prisoner of war from 1873 to 1880, first in Kazalinsk and later on in Kaluga in central Russia. According to popular conviction Muḥammad Murād was the one who was mainly to be blamed for the fall of Khiva (Samoilovich, 1909, 81).
[85] Ya'qūb bāy – one of the generals of the Khivan army (OIRUz-1, Nr. 9596, 476b-477a).
[86] Maḥmūd Niyāz – *yasāvulbāshī* (a military rank) – head of the guard at the court of Khiva (OIRUz-1, Nr. 9596, 476b; *Russkiĭ Invalid*, 1873, Nr. 5; Ivanov, 1940, 104, 125, 147).
[87] Qūngrāt – one of the administrative centers in the khanate of Khiva.
[88] 'Ibadallāh īshān – one of the religious authorities honored in Khiva. In the city a quarter and a *masjid* carry his name (Abdurasulov, 2000, 41, 52).

111. There is no other Axis in the world but you, there is no difference between good and bad today.
112. I bring the almighty Lord to intercede, be informed about the situation of the *murīdūn*.[89]
113. Your father and grandfather walked the Path, when they looked straight ahead, they made the mountains melt.
114. While looking at God's throne with the inner eyes, be informed about the situation of those who exert themselves. (256b)
115. Outward you are an old man, similar to an angel, day and night busy commemorating God.
116. Whose lamentations reach the Creator, be informed about the situation of the fortresses!
117. A great man always lives in great anguish for his country, may the Lord never expose us to such misfortunes!
118. The unbeliever came and circled the fortress three times, pray to the Lord and be our support!
119. There wouldn't be unbelievers, if we had remembered the Lord, be informed about the situation of those who have strayed!
120. He didn't become a slave to the almighty Lord, be informed about the situation of the ruler.
121. A green (flag)[90] was hoisted on the palace mosque, the unbeliever came and was shooting at it for twenty days.
122. The soldiers fled, our fortress did not burn down, now support the Muslims!
123. You know the Book of Judgment, become the leader of those who got lost!

---

[89] *Murīd*–disciple or adept of a *pīr* in Sufism.
[90] I.e. the flag of Islam.

124. The ruler cannot tell good from bad, be informed about the situation of thepoor people!
125. I constantly commemorate *sattār* and *jabbār*,[91] you are the only one left, oh Lord, possessing free will. (257a)
126. The descendants of Sheikh Mukhtār cry and moan,[92] be informed about everyone's situation!
127. The Lord's envoy, Jabrā'īl[93] was trustworthy and all your servants believe in you.
128. Khorezm is the prophet's possession, be informed about the situation of Khorezm.
The story about the damned unbelievers has come to an end here. All the others we wish a long life. May the life of our *pīr* the ruler last long and may he rise (against the Russians). Amen in the name of the Lord of both worlds.
The end. Written in 1296.
This book was finished on a Wednesday.
Remember the poor copyist in prayers, too.
(In Persian:) I am asking for a prayer said for me because I am a poor sinner.
Copied by Dāmullā Qurbān Niyāz.

---

[91] *Sattār*, *jabbār* : two of Allah's eminent qualities ("the Conceiling One", "the Almighty").

[92] Sheikh Mukhtār – one of the saints (d. 1288), honored in Khorezm. He was called *quṭb-i nāmdār* (Venerable Axis) (Babajanov, 2000, 151). His shrine is located 25 km east of Khiva, in the region of Yangi arik, in Astana village. Its construction is ascribed to Amir Kulāl (died in 1371) (Guliamov, 1941, 21). The marble plate of the grave points out that the sheikh died in 686/1287. He is considered the patron saint of the silk cultivators and the druggists (Rakhmonov, Yusupov, 1963, 11).

[93] Jabrā'īl – one of the four angels in Islam, who maintained the connection between God and the prophet.

# Text 2:

## *Munājāt* for the Russian tsar including wishes for victory in the Russo-Japanese war (1904)

### *Introduction*

The khanate of Khiva may have been a vassal of the Russian empire, but it kept its relative independence. The situation in the Turkestan governorate-general was slightly different. Beginning with the end of the 19th century ideas of reform made themselves felt; changes within the society became visible here. In the first instance, this can be traced in the views and attitudes of the Turkestan reformers – the well-known *jadīds*.[94] They united Eastern (=Islamic/Muslim) and Western achievements and values, out of which they intended to create a new culture. At the same time, traditional social currents that had been active for centuries also held their own. The reformers opened schools with new methods, where secular subjects were taught alongside theological ones. The final exams at the secondary school of ʿAbd al-Qādir Shakūrī (1875-1943) in Samarkand in the school year of 1912-13, for example, started with a religious part. Quotations from the Quran and religious books were read. At the same time a *munājāt* was recited.[95] But

[94] Baldauf, 2001; Khalid, 2000. - See also Franz Wennberg: *An Inquiry into Bukharan Qadīmism: Mīrzā Sālim-bīk.* Berlin 2002 (ANOR : 13). Translators' addition.

[95] Khalid, 2000, 172.

beside the innovations which the *jadīd* reformers consciously strove for, the traditional genres of medieval Islamic literature also started to change, for instance the *munājāt*. People began to see them as new vehicles for social mobilization.

Under the conditions of the Turkestan governorate-general (1867-1917), for example, the subject matter and the "beneficiary" of the requests in the *munājāt* started to undergo change. Over time, with the establishment of colonial rule, the peoples of Turkestan got used to the empire and the Russian tsar was accepted as the head of their own Islamic state, that is, the *pādishāh*.[96] Using the traditional literary genres as well, the Muslims endeavored to support their ruler, regardless of whether he was a Muslim himself or not. After the revolt led by Muḥammad ʿĀlī khalīfa, better known as Dukchī-īshān (1852-1898),[97] the local population (of Kokand, Osh and the Osh region) presented Nicolai II, the last Russian emperor (1894-1917), with so-called "Addresses" which typically consisted of praise for the Turkestan governor-general and severe criticism of Dukchī-īshān. These "Addresses" were published in both Uzbek and Russian.[98] In addition they also wrote *qaṣīdas* and translated them into Russian[99].

Such was the situation prevailing in 1904-05, when Russia fought its war with Japan. During this period a number of poems in Uzbek appeared in the Turkestani press which supported the Russian government and praised the

---

[96] Not without reason the Russian emperor was called "*āq pāshshā*" – the white ruler/tsar in Central Asia.

[97] Allworth, 1990, 118; Babajanov, 1998.

[98] TVG, 1898, Nr. 35; *Turkestanskie vedomosti*, 1898, Nr. 64.

[99] TVG, 1898, Nr. 40; *Turkestanskie vedomosti*, 1898, Nr. 68.

emperor:[100] "Good wishes for the Russian army, by the district administrator in Osh", "Good wishes to the sovereign, the emperor".[101] After this, on July 29, 1904, the popular poet from the Osh district, Mullā 'Umar Uzāq Imām Naẓar ughlī Faqīrī wrote a *munājāt* dedicated to the Russo-Japanese war which was published in the *Turkestan Vilayetining Gazeti*.[102] In it, the author asked the Almighty to support the Russian tsar and to help the Russians to gain victory over the enemy. In other words, about twenty-five years after the first *munājāt* under study here, where the poet requested God "With your power destroy the unbeliever!" (see above: this text was copied in Khiva in 1878 und possibly written earlier, perhaps during the conquest itself or shortly after), the direction of *munājāt*-writing and reciting swang to the opposite. The Muslim poet from the Turkestan governorate-general now used the following refrain-like formula: "*Har āfatīngīn asra ūl pādishāhīmīznī!*" (Save our *pādishāh* from any misfortune!) (in the Russo-Japanese war).

The authors of the quoted poems were nonprofessional popular poets, whose pseudonyms (*noms de plume*) are not mentioned in the known written sources (such as biographical dictionaries, anthologies and so on). The popular character of the texts is also evident from the rather low stylistic level of the poems. However, it seems that it was easier to propagate the idea of colonialism within the masses when local popular poets were put to the task, and the religious-spiritual genre (of the *munājāt*) seemed an appropriate instrument. In spirit, these

100 Zhalolov, Uzganboev, 1993, 28-30.

101 TVG, 1904, Nr. 24, 25.

102 TVG, 1904, Nr. 24,25.

*munājāt* are quite close to the official Russian imperial anthem "God save the Tsar!" (see below in the essay by N. P. Ostroumov). That means that the tsarist powers had succeeded in finding a literary genre in Islamic culture which was sufficiently close to the official one.

In the poem the author asks God to support the Russian tsar and to spare him from his (God's) punishment; he calls the tsar his protector. Apart from that, the tsar is called *pādishāh* of the Muslims: in him, the Muslims see their ruler. In the *munājāt* the name of the Russian ruler is not mentioned, only A. N. Kuropatkin is quoted (1848-1925). In his youth, he took part in the conquest of Central Asia. He later became the governor-general of Turkestan (1916-1917). From 1898 to 1917, A. N. Kuropatkin was Minister of War, and from October 13, 1904, until March 3, 1905, he commanded the armed forces in the Far Eastern theater of war. Later he was held responsible for the defeat and was dismissed from all positions.[103] The *munājāt* was dated July 29, 1904, hence

[103] *Uzbek sovet entsiklopediasi.* Vol. 6, Toshkent, 1975, 183. - The Russo-Japanese war started in February 1904; after some fighting done around Port Arthur (now Lü-Shun in Northeastern China on the Liaotung peninsula). The Russian aim was by no means to conquer Japan, but to consolidate Russian influence in Manchuria and to gain a position in Corea; the main reason for the war was the Russo-Japanese rivalry over these regions, and particularly the newly acquired Russian fortress at Port Arthur. The major events were the surrender of Port Arthur (January 2, 1905), the final battle of the land war at Mukden (February-March 1905) which saw Russian defeat amidst heavy casualties on both sides, and finally the naval battle of Tsushima (May 1905) where the Russian Baltic fleet which had made all the way to the Far East was completely crushed; this defeat prepared Russia for ending the war (September 1905). Since all the major events were still ahead, the analyzed text probably should not be taken to comment any particular Russian action, but rather be seen as a general encouragement for the Russian arms. No decisive naval battle was indeed fought until

at a time when A. Kuropatkin was Russian Minister of War. The author looks at him with hope also as supreme commander. Japan and the Japanese are depicted as both Russia's enemies, and the enemies of the Turkestani people. The poem voices a request to God to grant the ruler victory. Of course, the author, as a popular poet, could not understand the political significance of the war between Russia and Japan. However, he was convinced of one truth: the ruler, his very person guarantees stability and peace for the state. It was necessary to support the tsar – he was, after all, the ruler over all the Muslims in Turkestan. Of course, the whole poem could have been commissioned by the government. But one should not lose sight of the corresponding currents within Muslim society: for many, the preservation of the charismatic personality was a priority.

The *munājāt* consists of 7 stanzas, each of which has four lines (all in all 28 *bayts*) and, in contrast to the content, it formally does not differ much from the *munājāt* composed in Khiva. Here, we present the text of the *munājāt* together with its translation. Numbering of lines by the editor. The last paragraph is a comment by the editor of the newspaper.

---

Tsushima. The previous minor engagements, for all they showed Japanese superiority, did not result in any decisive advantages for the Japanese. In latter stages of the war, Muslim attitudes in the Russian Empire changed sharply, and the influence of this first victory of a non-European country over one of the European Powers on "native" thinking has often been stressed. - Translators' addition.

## Translation

## Munājāt *with good wishes*
## *Poem dedicated to the Russo-Japanese war*
## *By Mullā 'Umar Uzāq Imām Naẓar ughlī Faqīrī,*
## *Resident of the community of Tāshlāq*[104]
## *Situated in the Osh county of the Osh district*[105]

1. Lord, give our sovereign health,
2. Our supporter, our caring protector,
3. Our wise ruler, who brought the whole world into order,
4. Save our *pādishāh* from all misfortunes!
5. (He) who knows about the situation of the orphans, widows, unfortunates,
6. His justice renders impossible any kind of oppression,
7. Send immeasurable misfortunes upon his enemies,
8. Save our *pādishāh* from all misfortunes!
9. They say that the victor over the enemies gave battle at sea,
10. Lord Kuropatkin[106] fastened his belt tight,

---

[104] Tāshlāq – today, the region of Tashlak belongs to the republic of Uzbekistan.

[105] Osh – name of a town and region in the republic of Kirghizia.

11. The Russian forces intend to conquer Japan,
12. Save from misfortunes our *pādishāh*!
13. Give the Russian soldiers your assistance,
14. Send down burdens and agony on the Japanese army,
15. May the flash of misfortune strike the vermins of the world,
16. Save our *pādishāh* from all misfortunes!
17. May Russia show the Japanese a shattering stroke,
18. Lord, may she [Russia] conquer their cities with blessing!
19. May Russia extend its good deeds over the world
20. Save our *pādishāh* from all misfortunes!
21. The people of Osh and Andijan[107] always pray (for Russia),
22. And the people of Margilan, Kokand and Namangan,[108]
23. O Lord, accept the invocations of the Turkestani subjects,
24. Save our *pādishāh* from all misfortunes!
25. May my God show his grace to Russia,
26. May he benevolently accept the prayers of the Muslims,
27. May he grant Faqīrī's request all the time:
28. Save our *pādishāh* from all misfortunes!

---

[106] Kuropatkin – Kuropatkin, A. N. (1848-1925) – general of the infantry. At the time of the considered events, he was Russian Minister of War. See introduction to the translation.

[107] The inhabitants of Osh and Andijan - the population of two towns in the Ferghana valley which then was within the Turkestan governorate-general (1867-1917).

[108] Towns in the Ferghana valley.

The newspaper, in which we often write, can be compared to a mirror reflecting people's positive and negative features alike; we thus include into this issue the poems of this poet from Osh without any changes or corrections. In doing so, we of course hope that knowledgeable people will correct the deficiencies in rhythm, stanza and meter that these lines may carry. We have already once before written about the poems of a similar poet:

You wrote a poem in which nothing is as it should be:
One line short, the other three yards long.

# *Text 3:*

## *Khuṭba* for the Russian emperor And An essay of N.P. Ostroumov (1846-1930) about it

### Introduction

If the *munājāt* is a deeply personal (or even secret) prayer, its realization depending on the very personality of the author, the *khuṭba* on the other hand is a sermon officially intended for a broad audience.
In the papers left by the local historiographer N. Ostroumov which are deposited in the Central Government archive of the Republic of Uzbekistan the text of a *khuṭba* in Uzbek is preserved, written for the benefit of the Russian tsar Alexander II (1881-1894). It was composed more than fourteen years after the governorate-general of Turkestan had been established in 1867.[109] The text was written on a sheet of paper, measuring 18x27,5cm and glued on to a wooden plate of somewhat larger dimensions, 19,5x29cm. At its top, the plate carries a round loop, obviously intended to hang up the plate on the wall.[110] The considered text of the *khuṭba*

[109] The Turkestan governorate-general was established after the first wave of conquest of Central Asia on July 11, 1867, with its center and capital at Tashkent.
[110] TsAGRUz, *fond* Ostroumov, I-1009, opis' 1, delo 34, fol. 19. Unfortunately, there are no other documents about this text left in the file: the remaining documents concern other topics. See the text on the plate in the chapter on the first *khuṭba*.

has not attracted scholarly attention so far. In connection with this find, I looked through the complete archive of N. Ostroumov (all together 194 units). One of the units in the *fond* is titled "Prayer for the Russian tsar in Turkestan".[111] In this unit, I discovered an autograph essay by Ostroumov, the "Essay on the *khuṭba* for the Russian tsar". In this essay, Ostroumov explains the history of this sermon and its translation into "Sart" (Uzbek). He also addresses some peculiarities of the mentioned *khuṭba*. The text of the considered *khuṭba* with its translation (and its variant in the name of Nicolai II) is published here along with this essay by N. Ostroumov.

As is commonly known, the *khuṭba* is a particular form of sermon including prayers for the ruler, his health and long life, which is pronounced during Friday and holiday prayers.[112] In it, the *imām-khaṭīb* welcomes the assembled, praises God, asks the prophet Moḥammad for blessings, reads passages from the Quran, prays for the believers and guides them along the path of piety.[113] Sometimes *khuṭbas* are read on special occasions: to prevent natural catastrophes (draught, famine) or to celebrate victory over an enemy.[114] *Khuṭbas* of diverse thematic focus are known.[115]

---

[111] TsGARUz, fond I-1009, opis 1, delo 88, foll. 1-9.

[112] For example, "*Khuṭba-i yavm al-jum'a*" (OIRUz-1, Nr. 54/2, 29a (SVR, IV, Nr. 3435); "*Khuṭbat al-jum'a va-l-'īd*" (OIRUz-1, Nr. 3255/2, 311a-313b (SVR, IV, Nr. 3412); the anthology of *khuṭbas* (SVR, IV, Nr. 3440). By the way, during the Umayyad period (661-750), within the different prosaic literary genres, also rhetorical works were listed, among them the sermon – the *khuṭba* (Fil'shtinskii, 1985, 244).

[113] Khalidov, 1991.

[114] Bartol'd, 1966, 15-78; EI², V, 75-77 (Wensinck).

[115] Hutbe, 1950.

The *khuṭba* took on an important political role due to the following point: when praying for the believers, it was the *khaṭīb*'s duty to mention the ruling caliph by name, later this was extended to the rulers of regional states. In the second half of the 9$^{th}$ century individual regional rulers managed to have their name inserted after the name of the caliph. From that time on the mention in the *khuṭba* became one of the attributes by which the independence and sovereignty of a given ruler was formally expressed.[116] Based on that, each sovereign, after his enthronement, tried to enlarge and reinforce the legitimatory basis for his power by having his name mentioned in the Friday sermon. In that way he could hope to strengthen his authority.[117] Apart from the Friday sermon, he focused his attention on the *sikka* (coinage; on Muslim coins, the name of the ruler also is inscribed as a general rule). Both elements were at once instruments and the main attributes to confirm the ruler's enthronement and his legitimacy.[118]

The *khuṭba*, as is well known, has already been the subject of scholarly research at least partly, but not completely; for instance, the material from Central Asia still remains unexplored together with the history of the literary genre in the region and the various political contexts in which it could be used.[119] In that sense it is

[116] Khalidov, 1991.

[117] Khalid, 2000, 34.

[118] On *sikka* see: EI$^2$, IX, 614-624. The history of Central Asia is abundant with examples of readings of *khuṭbas* in favor of the ruler: Abū-l-Faḍl Bayhaqī, 1969, 75, 117, 130,...; Shihāb ad-dīn Muḥammad an-Nasavī, 1973, 38, 46, 57,...; *Le livre de Babur*, 1985, 34; Fāṣiḥ Aḥmad, 1980, 41, 79, 92, ...; Maḥmūd ibn Valī, 1977, 16.

[119] In that case, of course, if one excludes Ostroumov's essay, in which he, to a certain point, consulted the Central Asian material. Manuscript *khuṭba* anthologies of Central Asian origin: texts of the *khuṭba* in

hoped that the essay by N. Ostroumov and the two texts of *khuṭbas* published here can offer some of the materials needed in this respect.

Originally, the *khuṭba* was said in Arabic. Among Muslims outside the Arab world, however, a departure from this tradition is evident.[120] The considered *khuṭba* is written in Uzbek. The colonial administration bore in mind that, no matter how strong the religiousness of the local population might be, the people did not understand religious Islamic texts in Arabic and had no way of grasping what was being said in neither texts nor sermons. Thus, the tsarist administration made use of this religious-spiritual genre for its purposes and had it transposed into the local language. With the help of this text it was easier to legitimate the own presence among the local Muslims. On the other hand, the considered genre had a straight political context, throwing up the question of the ruling sovereign. For this reason "during the colonial period the powers indirectly interfered with the contents of the *khuṭba*."[121]

There is another circumstance which immediately catches one's eye. The object of the *khuṭba* is the Russian emperor. He is the colonizer, but most important of all, he is not a Muslim. Moreover, in a Turkestani *khuṭba* it was necessary to pray for the emperor's family, too – for

---

Arabic (OIRUz-1, Nr. Nr. 2992/XII; 3080; 3095; 4144; 4188/XI). One of those anthologies is dedicated to the last ruler of Bukhara of the Manghit dynasty (1747-1920), the "*Khuṭba ba-nām-i amīrān-i Bukhārā*" (OIRUz-1, Nr. 12793/III, 33b-50b). See also: *Handlist*, 2000, 13, 26, 101, 220, 272. Manuscripts in other depositories: *Arabskie rukopisi*, 1986, 180-182.

[120] EI², V, 77.

[121] Khalidov, 1991.

the empress and the crown prince.[122] Thus, the tsarist powers wanted to raise a feeling of respect for the complete tsarist house. The tsarist family always had to stay in public attention for all peoples in the empire.[123]
In 1897 for example, that is one year before the in Andijan uprising in 1898, a commission of the tsarist power visited its future epicenter – the settlement of Mingtipa. The members of the commission met the leader of the future rebellion, Muḥammad ʿAlī khalīfa (1852-1898),[124] better known among the people by his epithet Dukchī-īshān. His growing authority disturbed the tsarist powers.[125] It is interesting to note that the official in charge of the mission spoke about the power of the Russian tsar during the conversation or rather interrogation he conducted with Dukchī-īshān, and he expressed the wish that the īshān and his followers should memorize the names of the family of the tsar.[126]
However, not all accepted the high and respectful attitude to the imperial family which was actually being

---

[122] One of those prayers, published in Kazan in 1887, is titled "*Duʿā-nāma*". It was written in Arabic in the name of the Russian emperor Alexander III (1881-1894) and contains a request to God for the health of the emperor and his family. This sermon was added as a supplement to the publication "*Khulāṣat al-masāʾil*" (OIRUz, fond litografii, Nr. 11068, 268).

[123] E.g.: the very same N. Ostroumov emphasized in an editor's report about the newspaper "*Turkestan vilāyatīning gazīti*" ("Turkestanskaia tuzemnaia gazeta") which he addressed to the *kantseliariia* of the Turkestan governor-general that the newspaper acted in complete harmony with its guidelines. Ten basic subject matters were enumerated which formed the main body of its publications. Among the permanent and main topics "Short reports on the life of the Russian ruling house..." (Ernazarov, Akbarov, 1976, 20) held the first place.

[124] Allworth, 1990, 118; Babajanov, 1998, 167-191.

[125] TVG, 30.3.1896, Nr.12.

[126] Fozilbek Otabek ugli, 1992, 17-19.

forced on them with equal joy, even though the *khuṭba* was used with just this in mind. In 1910 the Kokand poetess 'Anbar-Ātūn (1870-1915) wrote the philosophical work "*Risāla-yi falsafa-yi siyāhān*" ("Treatise on the philosophy of the blacks"). One character in this text criticizes the mullahs, and among other things he states that they mention the tsar after the name of God, his messenger and the four rightly-guided caliphs in their *khuṭbas*, and that this could easily be seen as veneration (*sajda*; literally: prosternation, an act Muslims reserve for God) of the tsar. The character cries out his refusal to venerate the "White Tsar" in this way.[127]

Those mullahs who formed the conformist wing of the Islamic clergy, who composed *khuṭbas* with prayers in favor of the Russian tsar at the end got into a delicate situation themselves,[128] since what they were doing amounted to the Islamic ulama's legitimizing the power of the "unbelievers".

One should not forget the psychological and cultural aspects of the problem. For centuries, the peoples of Central Asia had been living under various monarchic regimes. In their mindset, the *khuṭba* in the name of the ruler was the natural form for legitimizing (or even consecrating) the power that be. Now, the new power was a power of unbelievers. But even this circumstance did not keep a part of the Muslims (and evidently, a significant number, not just a small minority of collaborators) from accepting the Russian tsar as "their" ruler. And in fact, there was no other ruler in what now was the Russian governorate-general of Turkestan since

---

127 Dilshod, Anbar Otin, 1994, 169.

128 Babajanov, 1998, 167.

the khanate of Kokand had ceased to exist in February 1876.

In the year 1930, the year of his death, N. Ostroumov focused on the composition of a *khuṭba* in the name of the tsar and wrote an interesting polemic essay about its history. His text has been preserved in the TsGARUz, in the Ostroumov *fond*: I-1009, op. 1, delo 88. The manuscript consists of nine folios, writing is on both sides, measures 17,5x21,5, blue ink; very tiny hand.

The author of the essay, Nikolai Petrovich Ostroumov, was a pedagogue who had finished the spiritual academy of Kazan in the "Anti-islamic department" (1866-70). In 1877 he moved to Tashkent. But he did not take up work as a missionary because the tsarist government was very much reserved about missionaries in Turkestan. Ostroumov started as a writer and journalist. As local historiographer, N. Ostroumov studied many sides of Muslim life.[129] He published a number of works on Islam and the culture of the Turkic nations, in particular the Uzbeks.[130] But all the same, he did not forget his former profession: in 1885-86 he edited a translation of the Gospel into Uzbek.[131] During that period he also wrote a polemical work, polemicizing against the Quran: "Quran and progress".[132] He worked as a teacher, after that he became the director of the teachers' seminary in Turkestan. At the same time, in 1883-1917, he became the

[129] On N. Ostroumov's works see: *Spisok*, 1920; *Istoriografiia*, 1974, 259-271.

[130] See a number of his works on oriental studies: Ostroumov, 1876; 1877; 1883; 1896; 1901; 1908; 1910; 1910-1914; 1911; *Araviia i Koran*, 1899; *Materialy*, 1899; *Materialy*, 1917; *Perevod iarlyka*, 1917.

[131] The translation was printed in Leipzig (*Istoriografiia*, 1974, 261).

[132] Ostroumov, 1901. He paid special attention to the Quran: Ostroumov, 1883;1900.

editor of the official newspaper in Uzbek, "*Turkistān vilāyatīning gazītī*" (1870-1917).[133] He was familiar with local dialects and mores, all of which gained him great respect among the local population. Parallel to those activities he became the vice-president of the Turkestan circle of amateur archeologists (1895-1917).[134] N. Ostroumov was a difficult and contradictory figure.[135]
N. Ostroumov personally conducted research on the topic in question here and laid down his lifelong observations in the essay. On top of that he knew the rules of Islam, was well acquainted with the mindset dominant among the local population. It was maybe for that reason that he reacted so sharply to the text of the *khuṭba* which had been composed in honor of the Russian ruler; his main point being that the given text did not correspond to what a *khuṭba* is about: it is a sermon pronounced for a Muslim ruler.[136] But on another level, we should keep in mind that the essay was composed in 1930, a period when the Soviet atheist battle which had been raging for a while was approaching its climax. This of course meant that the situation had changed dramatically since the beginning of the 20th century.

---

[133] The considered newspaper at first was published as a supplement ("*Ilovalar*") to "*Turkestanskie vedomosti*" (1870-1917) – the official paper of the tsarist administration in Turkestan. From 1883 these supplements became an independent newspaper – "*Turkestan vilāyatīning gazītī*" (TVG).

[134] On that circle see: Lunin, 1958.

[135] He was no academic scholar, but a provincial orientalist. The famous orientalist I. Yu. Krachkovskiy (1883-1951) characterized him as a "great scholar of the local area", and V. V. Bartol'd (1869-1930) called him the "patriarch of Turkestan studies" (*Istoriografiia*, 1974, 260-61).

[136] Ostroumov published a number of condolence poems, dedicated to the Russian sovereign, that were composed by locals (Ostroumov, 1896).

Having his own opinions on the question, N. Ostroumov studied the sources and history of composing prayers for the Russian ruler in Turkestan.[137] In a wide overview over the history of the question, he quoted some examples of similar *khuṭbas* and prayers in honor of rulers pronounced by representatives of other religions (basing himself on Central Asian material).

N. Ostroumov understood very well that the text of the *khuṭba* proposed to the administration neither matched the mentality of the local believers, nor, more importantly, the "political and spiritual status" which was claimed for the Russian ruler. That was why he suggested a variant of the text with the help of his Muslim friends among the local intellectuals which he thought was more likely to agree with the conception of the Muslims. All that was done with the approval of the governor-general A. B. Vrevskii.[138] Criticizing the existing text of the *khuṭba*, N. Ostroumov suggested his own variant, which was "more likely to correspond to the Muslim spirit".[139]

There is no hard evidence so far to prove that the sermon under study was actually employed in practice, or more precisely, whether it was read in mosques and Russo-native schools. N. Ostroumov had his doubts about that and instead maintained that it was read in the Russo-native schools only.[140] But at the same time he did not

---

[137] He used his observations and material from his archive for his essay: "*The present essay was composed in 1930, on the basis of notes in my diary and a number of publications and articles, written in the 20th century*" (TsGARUz, fond I-1009, opis' 1, delo 88, fol.1a).

[138] Vrevskii, A. B. – governor-general of the Turkestan region (1889-1898).

[139] See: first *khuṭba*.

[140] Russo-native schools – Russian schools in Turkestan for teaching Muslim children. Interpreters were schooled and trained there. These

reject the further use of the *khuṭba* in Tatar in the regional schools as apparently had been previous practice.

In 1894, after the death of Alexander III, Nicolai II succeeded him on the throne. Immediately after the beginning of the new reign, another *khuṭba* was published in the local official newspaper (mentioned above) with the names changed in favor of Nicolai II.[141] Beneath the text there is a note concerning its purpose: "for obligatory reading in the mosques of Turkestan province and the Russo-native schools on high holidays".

During the first half of the 1890s an inspection was held in the Islamic schools. At the time of this inspection the school administration succeeded in implementing one change only: the "Prayer for the tsar" was read in the schools in Uzbek (rather than Tatar).[142] That means that up to that point the *khuṭba* had been read in Tatar in the Turkestani madrasas. But for the time being, we do not know whether or not this particular *khuṭba* was used henceforth. The observations of N. Ostroumov might provide precious material on the history of prayer in Central Asia.

The author provided his essay with many footnotes, which I included in the main text within brackets and marked them in italic; they are introduced by two asterisks. All underlined words and sentences in the essay were emphasized by N. Ostroumov himself.

---

schools existed form 1884-1917. In 1917 there were 170 such schools, 84 of them on the territory of present-day Uzbekistan (Bendrikov, 1960).

[141] TVG, 25.11.1894, Nr.43. See: second *khuṭba*.

[142] Bendrikov, 1960, 74.

*Text 3.1*

## Translation

## Ostroumov N. P.
## The history of the "prayer for the Tsar", meant for being read in the mosques of Tashkent and Russo-native schools

(*** *The present essay was composed in 1930, on the basis of my diary and a number of publications and articles I wrote during the 20th century*)

Two circumstances conducted me to undertake the composition of this essay.

On Wednesday, March 3, 1892, in the 9th issue of the "Turkestanskie vedomosti" I read a note which I quote here: "His Excellency the commander-in-chief of the region ("" *Baron Alexander Borisovich Vrevskiy. – N.O.*) considered inevitable that in the Muslim mosques throughout Turkestan, the members of the constituency say prayers for the health and long life of His Majesty the Emperor and His Highness the Crown prince, Tsesarevich, on the following holidays: anniversary of His Imperial Majesty's inthronisation, as well on the birthdays of Their Imperial Majesties the Emperor and His Highness the Crown prince, further on New Year's Days according to the Islamic calendar[143]. The text of this prayer has been elaborated by an assembly of national

[143] I.e. the new year according to the Islamic lunar calendar.

judges[144] of the city of Tashkent and was confirmed by his Excellency, the commander-in-chief of Turkestan region, as follows:

"Our Lord! Help, show mercy to His Majesty the Sovereign our Alexander Alexandrovich[145] as well as his spouse Empress Maria Fedorovna[146] and the Crown prince (1b), His Highness the Tsesarevich Nicolai Alexandrovich[147] and the other Imperial children. Amen.

Our Lord! Make the Tsar merciful for all his subjects and let him rule over us eternally. Amen.

Our Lord! Save the Tsar and His spouse together with the Imperial family from heavenly and worldly misfortune, from human envy and evildoings. Amen.

Our Lord! Extend the life of the Tsar and make Him and His family rule over us eternally. Amen.

Our Lord! Make His birthday and coronation anniversary sacred days to us. Amen.

Our Lord! Save also His worthy ministers, loyal followers, faithful defenders of the state, and give Him continuous victory over his enemies. Amen.

Our Lord! May His chosen governors act according to His orders. Amen.

Our Lord! May everybody thrive under His wise guidance: high and low, men and women. Amen."" (2a)

I was interested in the decree issued by baron Vrevskii, and some of the expressions used in the text of the prayer caused my utter bewilderment. I discussed the matter with the Head inspector of schools and asked him to

[144] I.e. the Islamic judge (*qāḍī*).

[145] Tsar Alexander III (1845-1894) – Russian emperor 1881-1894.

[146] Maria Fedorovna – the wife of Alexander III.

[147] Nicolai Alexandrovich – Nicolai II (1868-1918), son of Alexander III. Nicolai II was the last Russian emperor (1894-1917).

report this to the governor-general. After actually agreeing on the basic idea of the mentioned decree, I explained to Kerenskii,[148] that the Quran does not in the least recommend Muslims to have a good and friendly relations with Christians (** *"O ye who have believed, do not choose Jews and Christians as friend;" (Christians)*[149] *Surah 5;56*[150] *And in another Surah of the Quran "Let not the Believers take the Unbelievers as friends in preference to the Believers; if anyone does that, he is not of Allah's party at all;"(Surah 3;27,*[151] *also Surah 4;143). Muḥammad*[152] *issued these and other summons to call his contemporaries to fight the unbelievers; but later on, the Muslims referred to these sayings whenever questions arose about the relationship between believers and unbelievers. Such clashes occurred during the first centuries and after whenever Muslim rulers confronted not only Christian, but also unbelieving rulers in general. This is very evident in the material collected by V. Tizengauzen in his anthology on the history of the Golden Horde (St. Petersburg, 1884, chapter 1, p.98ff, and other well known Arab authors quoted in the same anthology*) and because of that it would be necessary to deal with the religious feelings of the natives more carefully. The natives, after all, were subdued by the arms

---

[148] Kerenskii – F. M. Kerenskii (1849-1912), high-ranking official ("deistvitel'nyi statskii sovetnik"). From 1889-1910 he was the head inspector of schools in the Turkestan region, a leading figure in society and politics, father of A. F. Kerenskii (1881-1970) – Russian politician.

[149] The word in brackets – "Christian" after "*Jews and Christian*" was added by N. Ostroumov; the original has *naṣārā* "Nazarenes" which usually is understood as Christians.

[150] See Bell, 101. The Russian translation used by Ostroumov was G.S. Sablukov's which was printed in Kazan' in 1907.

[151] see Bell, 47

[152] *Muḥammad*, the prophet.

of unbelievers, and their uneasiness over the continuing Russian rule had already made itself felt, particularly after the addition of Ferghana to Russia (*** *The events surrounding the Ferghana Muslim armed rebellion against the Russian army camp in Andijan, May 1898, are intended here. See also in the brochure by P. Galuzo "Turkestan as a colony" - Moscow, 1929*). From this point of view I thought it unconvincing to force the natives to pray for eternal rule of the Russian Tsar and his continuous victory over the enemies, in the first line of which stood the neighboring Islamic khanates of Central Asia. The Afghan khan ʿAbd ar-Raḥmān[153] used the support of the Turkestan (2b) administration and swore loyalty to general Kaufman[154] when he was still a pretender for the Afghan throne, but when he had occupied Afghanistan he did not show any good will for the Russians (see his report, translated into Russian by colonel Grulev).[155] The Quran not only forbids the Muslims friendship and love for the unbelievers, even though they (?...) are relatives (Surah 58;22),[156] but also

[153] ʿAbd al-Raḥmān – amīr of Afghanistan (1880-1901), from the Barakzai clan. He lived in Russia for quite a long time.

[154] Kaufman – K. P. fon Kaufman (1818-1882) the governor-general of the Turkestan krai (1867-1882); military leader of the conquest of Central Asia (see on him: MacKenzie, 1967; Siscoe, 1968).

[155] Here he speaks about the translation of ʿAbd al-Raḥmān's book into Russian, and his memories (see: *Abdurakhman-khan emir Afganistana. Avtobiografiia Abdurakhman-khan emira Afganistana.* Published by Sultan Magomet khan. Translation from English by Grulev. Vol. 1,2. Sankt- Peterburg, 1901). M. Grulev was a colonel of the general staff of the Russian army and is the author of the book "*Sopernichestvo Rossii i Anglii v Srednei Azii*" (Sankt- Peterburg, 1909).

[156] N. Ostroumov quotes the general idea of the Surah. Some passages of the quotation are impossible to read. The part of the Surah which N. Ostroumov focuses on here reads: "One does not find a people who believe in Allah and the Last Day in friendly relations with any who

prescribes to be strict with them, fight them and beat them without pity. That way Muslims would not be subject to temptation by the unbelievers, particularly regarding the one God and his Prophet, Muḥammad. In this context two sayings are noteworthy: "O our Lord, lay not upon us what we are not capable of bearing; pardon us and forgive us, and have mercy upon us; Thou art our patron, so help us against the people of unbelievers." (Surah 2;286).[157] Another saying states: "We are quit of you and of what ye serve apart from Allah, we renounce you, and there has appeared between us and you enmity and hatred for ever until ye believe in Allah alone" (Surah 60;4).[158]

Keeping in mind these quotations, I really wonder how the official representatives of Islam, the cadis,[159] were able to introduce into the text of a prayer a passage in which God is requested to grant the Russian tsar constant victory over his enemies ... Still doubtful about the sincerity of the prayer for the Russian tsar (whoever composed it), I find myself in an inconvenient situation, because I, as the editor (3a) of the local newspaper, was obliged to translate it into the local dialect[160] and publish

obstruct Allah and His messenger, even though they were their fathers, or their sons or their brethren or their clan; as for those, He hath inscribed faith on their hearts, and has supported them with a Spirit from Himself, and He will cause them to enter Gardens through which the rivers flow, therein to abide, Allah satisfied with them and they with Him. These are the party of Allah. Lo, verily the party of Allah are the ones who prosper."(see Bell, 566-567) (Koran. Translation from Arabic by G. S. Sablukov. Kazan, 1907).

157 See Bell, 42.

158 See Bell, 573.

159 I.e. cadi – Islamic judge, executing the jurisdiction on basis of the sharīʿa.

160 I.e. Uzbek.

the mentioned prayer. I also had to send it to the madrasas and the native officials through the regional head offices. Thus, the situation put me into an unfavorable role: I had to participate in the distribution of an inopportune decree issued by the governor-general concerning a sermon which, in my opinion, does not express the actual feelings of the natives. Moreover, I vividly recalled how baron Vrevskii's predecessor, governor-general Rozenbakh,[161] unfortunately attempted to have a prayer read for the tsar according to the "*Kazanskii sbornik*" (Khutbalyk)[162] in the Khodja-Ahrar mosque[163] on June 29, 1888. (** *The occasion for this was General Rozenbakh's official handing over of the mentioned mosque to the representatives of the native population. The Mosque had been reconstructed with funds which Tsar Alexander III had donated to the Emir*

---

[161] Rozenbakh – N. O. Rozenbakh, governor-general of the Turkestan krai (1884-1888). During his tenure the Russo-native schools were established (1884-1917) (Khalid, 2000, 157).

[162] Khutbalyk – a book (manual) on sermons, published in Kazan in Tatar. See also the Kazan publication of different *khuṭbas*: *Khuṭba Ādam 'alayhi l-salām khāṣṣiyatlarī birlan.* Qāzān, 1881; 1903; 1912 (OIRUz, fond litigrafii Nr. Nr. 5411, 5412; 12783). According to doctor D. Usmanova the following lithographic publication is preserved in the Kazan state university: Amashev (ed.), *Khuṭba-i jum'a.* Qāzān, 1878. We can add the following Turkestani publications: *Khuṭbāt.* Kāgān, 1905; *Khuṭba-i nikāḥ.* Toshkent, 1906 (OIRUz, fond litografii Nr. Nr. 11126; 14163).

[163] The Khoja Ahrar mosque – Khoja Aḥrār (1404-1490) was close to the Timurid rulers of his time, particularly those based at Samarkand. He was an important representative of the *Khojagan-Naqshbandiyya* sufi movement. - See J. Paul: *Die politische und soziale Bedeutung,* quoted above, and recently Jo-Ann Gross, Asom Urunbaev: *The letters of Khwāja 'Ubaid Allāh Aḥrār and his Associates.* Leiden 2002, with further references. Translators' addition.

*of Bukhara*[164] *on the occasion of his coronation. This ceremony had been described in "Turkestanskie vedomosti" (Nr. 33, August 23, 1888) in a report written in the style of an official government proclamation; the publication thus did not offer a true picture of the event which was so important in the lives of the Tashkent natives).*

Kerenskii submitted the information I had given to baron Vrevskii, who agreed to have changed the text of the prayer which he had already confirmed and which the cadis had approved. Kerenskii instructed me to compose another text, translate the new one and, when the local cadis had again given their consent, present it to the governor-general for distribution. (3b) The new text of the prayer in favor of the tsar which I composed was then translated with the help of my assistant at the newspaper, the former cadi, Sattar-khan ʿAbd al-Gafarov.[165] On 24th April 1892, the cadi of Tashkent, Muḥyiddīn-khoja,[166]

---

[164] From 1868 on the khanate of Bukhara was a vassal of Russia. In 1888 the amīr ʿAbd al-Aḥad khān (1885-1910) governed in Bukhara. He had very close relations to Alexander III (*Uzbekistonning yangi tarikhi*, 2000, 212).

[165] Sattarkhan Abdugafarov – S. Abdugafarov (1843-1901) was an important Turkestani enlightener and historian. He worked in the mentioned newspaper from 1883-1890 (see: A. N. Savitskii, *Sattarkhan Abdulgafarov –prosvetitel'-demokrat.* Tashkent, 1965). He published an essay on the Russian language in the khanate of Kokand (see: *Turkestanskie vedomosti*, 1892-93). His memoirs were published by N. Ostroumov (Ostroumov, 1896, 190-234).

[166] Mukhiddin-khoja - Muḥyī-d-Dīn Khoja (1840-1902). A famous cadi from Tashkent, son of the Tashkent *qāḍī-kalān* Ḥakīm Khoja. He was a close acquaintance of N. Ostroumov's (see: Ostroumov, *Mukhammed-Mukhitdin-Khoja.* In: *Turkestanskie vedomosti*, 1902, Nr. 28; Yusupov, *Furkat yullarida.* Toshkent, 1983).

approved the translation (s. details in my diary notes).[167] After this the prayer for the tsar and the ruling house was printed once more in a new version, and separate copies[168] were distributed to the Turkestan mosques and to the Russo-native school by native officials for being read on the corresponding holidays. The pupils of the Russo-native schools (sons of the natives of Tashkent) learnt the text of this prayer by heart like ordinary reading material, the Russian Imperial anthem,[169] and recited it in chorus whenever Russian leading personalities visited the school. Especially on the occasion of final exams, the schools were visited by the governor-general, the district governor, the city major, by representatives of schools and the native population and the parents of the participants. But whether the prayer was read in the mosques on Fridays and the tsarist holidays I doubt, even though the native representatives normally did declare to the governor-general on the military parades which were held on the so called "Tsarist days",[170] that on those very days, (actually they said "always") the prayer for the tsar and the ruling

---

[167] In the archive of Ostroumov there is a *delo* in which his diary (until 1894), written on single sheets of paper is preserved (I-1009, opis' 1, delo 67). The notes of the diaries from 1892 are extant down to April 17. Unfortunately, the notes after April 17 till the end of the year (January 1, 1893) are missing. Obviously, this part of the diary got lost.

[168] Most probably, as mentioned in another text, this *khuṭba* is the same separate copy, stuck to a plate which I mentioned at the very beginning of the introduction to the essay of Ostroumov. See second text of appendix.

[169] I.e. the official tsarist hymn of Russia "*Bozhe, tsaria khrani!*" (God Save the Tsar).

[170] The so called tsarist days are listed at the beginning of the essay.

house was read in the mosques (see the notes in my diary).[171]

It would seem now that there is no more to say about the question of how the prayer had been introduced. But our correspondent, who chose to veil his identity behind the letter D., had a note published in the newspaper "*Russkaya zhizn*", issue Nr. 109, April 23,1892 under the heading "Prayer for the tsar in Turkestan" which I quote here:[172] (4a)[173]

"In "*Novoe vremya*", Nr. 5780 (April 1) we read that the governor-general of Turkestan ordered the members of the constituencies to read a prayer in the regional mosques for the health of His Imperial Majesty and the crown prince Tsesarevich on holidays as well as on New Year's Day. The newspaper adds that the text of the prayer had been elaborated by an assembly of native judges of the city of Tashkent and had been approved by the governor-general.

This information is not completely exact and needs to be corrected. Such a decree had already been issued in the year 1888 under the following circumstances. At the time of the latter's coronation (1883) the Sovereign the Emperor gave the Emir of Bukhara a present of 30 000 rubles in Bukharan currency. It pleased the ruler to order that the money be spent for the needs of the Turkestan region – and, according to His Majesty's pleasure, the local authorities earmarked this sum for the reconstruction of some especially venerated mosques.

---

[171] Unfortunately I couldn't identify these notes.

[172] The given note is a cutting from the newspaper, added to Ostroumov's manuscript at fol. 4.

[173] Fol. 4b is empty.

Thus, the mosque Sultan-Azret,[174] unique in its dimensions, was reconstructed, - after that the ancient mosque in the village of Zangi Ata (15 kilometers from Tashkent)[175] and the mosque named after Khoja Aḥrar[176] in Tashkent were repaired. The latter was then called "the Tsarist" among the local population.[177] On July 29, 1888, the former governor-general Rozenbakh handed over the mosque to the mullahs and cadis in a ceremonial setting and on the same date, a prayer was held in the mosque for His Majesty the tsar, the Crown prince and the whole Ruling House.

As far as I know, this prayer was not composed by anyone, but its form was authorized [by the "*Kazanskii sbornik*"] and it only had to be translated from the Kazan dialect of Tatar into Sart. After that the prayer was read on every Islamic holiday (Friday).

---

[174] Sultan-Azret – Khoja Aḥmad Yasavī (died in 562/1166-67) was a famous mystic, founder of the *ṭarīqa yasaviyya*. The *masjid* (more precisely a shrine) was built in 1389 at the place of his death on Temur's orders (1380-1405). Temur visited this shrine before his campaigns (B. Albaum, *Herren der Steppe*. Berlin, 1976, 96; T. Nagel, *Timur der Eroberer und die islamische Welt des späten Mittelalters*. München, 1993, 416). - The dates of Aḥmad Yasavī need to be corrected in the light of Devin DeWeese's work; and for the actual situation at the shrine, see Privratsky's book quoted above. - Translators' edition.

[175] Zangi Ata (died in 1258) – a Sufi saint of the *yasaviyya* order (J. S. Trimingem, *Sufiiskie ordeny v islame*. Moskva, 1989, 57-59; that is J. S. Trimingham: *Sufi Orders in Islam*. Oxford 1971, dated in a number of details, translators' addition). The *masjid* and shrine of Zangi Ata are located 16 km south of Tashkent.

[176] I.e. the *masjid* named after Khoja Aḥrār.

[177] A very curious circumstance: the believers and the imam of the *masjid* Khoja Aḥrār, when taking over the reconstructed mosque, were supposed to express somehow how much they thanked the person who donated such an immense sum for its reconstruction. Perhaps that is the reason the mosque received the name "Tsarist", following its donator.

Perhaps, the decree about praying for the Tsar in mosques was actually issued even before 1888 – but I have no information about that.

D."

Supplementing the published note, another Muslim provided me with a short explanation in defense of the Muslims of inner Russia, who, as the author of the note recalls, found it necessary to pray in the mosque for His Majesty the Emperor each Friday. Here is his explanation:[178]

اعوذ بالله من الشيطان الرجيم     واطيعو الرسول و الوا الامير

„O obey God, his Prophet, and those in Power (Surah 4;62) (** *The author tried to cite an Arabic text from the Quran (Surah 4;62), but why didn't he complete the last words "among you", which means from among the Muslims. He didn't note either where the Sharia mentions the necessity for Muslims to pray for unbelieving rulers...* N.O.).[179]
In the Sharia book it is said that the Sharia orders to love the homeland, which nourishes and be [unreadable; conjecture: loyal to that person] (without difference of

[178] The text of the explanation is written in a different hand on a separate sheet of paper, measuring 16,5x22 and glued to Ostroumov's manuscript.

[179] The complete text of the outlined Surah (4:62) reads as follows: "O ye who have believed, obey Allah and obey the messenger and those of you who have the command, and if ye quarrel about anything, refer it to Allah and the messenger, if ye have come to believe in Allah and the Last Day; that is better and fairer in interpretation." (Bell, 77.) – The introduction of the quotation is a pious formula which is often used whenever Muslims quote from the Quran. The last word should read *amr* instead of *amīr*. – Translators' addition.

nation and belief) who offers protection. The Russian ulama interpret and explain this last regulation of the Sharia differently, and I remember, they found it necessary to pray for the Russian tsar, and for that reason, in every Russian mosque, every week on Fridays after the holiday prayer (jumʿa), the mullah asks the praying to pray for His Imperial Majesty, and then the prayer finishes." (5a)

I find the published note of the correspondent D. and the handwritten explanation of the other Muslim equally insufficient, because both do not give an exact answer to the main question: who was the first to make the Russian and Turkestan Muslims think that they have to pray for the Russian tsar, despite his disbelief, and when did that happen? The author of the published note, D. said, that "this prayer wasn't composed by anyone (!), but its form was authorized by the law", but moreover, he did not indicate which authorization and which law he had in mind and did not make clear whether the text which the Tashkent cadis composed accorded to the rules laid down by that law... . The writer who sent me the handwritten note tried to quote a verse from the Quran in his letter, (Surah 4;62), but left out the suffix pronoun "from among you", actually, in Russian translation this verse must be read as follows: "O ye who have believed, obey Allah and obey the messenger and those of you who have the command."[180] This means that the Quran ordered the Muslims to obey, apart from God and Muḥammad, also the powerful Muslims, but without the pronoun of you the sense of the cited saying changes in so far that now the first Muslims were ordered to obey their rulers in general, whether they belonged to their religion or not.

[180] See Bell, p. 75.

For that reason, the Russian ulama differently interpreted and explained the Sharia rulings concerning love for the home country, and thus, they acknowledged the necessity for Muslims to pray for the tsar. But this explanation stands in obvious contrast to the literal sense of the Quranic saying. Nevertheless, Muslim writers quote this text as proof for the loyalty of the Russian Muslim subjects, as was the case in 1898, when governor-general Dukhovskii[181] led the investigation into the unprecedented assault on the camp of Andijan[182] by the Ferghana Muslims. When, in a published note, I pointed out that the pronoun "of you" had been left out in the quotation of the quranic text (4;62) as printed in Gasprinskii's newspaper[183], the Caucasian mufti[184] wrote to general Dukhovskii about his dissatisfaction caused by my note referring to the order of first class that he had been awarded by the Sovereign for true and loyal service. The correspondent D. narrated that the prayer for the tsar, the Crown prince and the complete ruling (5b) house had first been held on July 29, 1888 in the Khoja Aḥrār mosque in Tashkent, in presence of governor-general Rozenbakh and other leading personalities of the

[181] S. M. Dukhovskii – governor-general of the Turkestan krai (1898-1901).

[182] I.e. the Andijan rebellion in 1898.

[183] I. Gasprinskii (1851-1914) – founder of the reformist movement of the Jadids in the Russian empire. Here the newspaper is meant which he founded and published under the title of "Tarjuman" (lit. "Translator") (from 1883 on). Parts of the correspondence between Gasprinskii and Ostroumov are extant. (Khalid, 2000, 87).

[184] The Caucasian mufti – i.e. the Transcaucasian mufti from 1881-1917 was the Azerbaijan enlightener Husain-afandi Gaibov (1830-1917). (*Azerbaijan sovet ensiklopediiasy.* III jild, Baky, 1979, 5). He was the editor of the literary anthology of poems of famous Azerbaijan poets (publication: *Azerbaijanda meshhur olan shu'aranin esh'aridir.* Vol. I, Baku, 1986; II, 1989).

city, as described in issue 33 of the "*Turkestanskie vedomosti*", 1888 (***I was also present at the celebration and declare here that the description of the events as given in issue 33 of the "Turkestanskie vedomosti" had the character of an official bulletin*) and after that (supposedly) was carried out every Friday (in the Friday mosques of Tashkent, it is to be understood). "Perhaps", adds D., the correspondent, the decree about the reading of prayers for the tsar in Tashkent mosques was issued earlier than in 1888, but (to him) nothing is known... As a long-time resident of Tashkent, I can make the following statement on these matters: When the natives of Tashkent turned to the first Turkestani governor-general Kaufman, asking him for a cannon to be fired as salute on the first day of the highest Muslim holiday *(ʿīd al-fiṭr)* in order to mark and publicize the ending of the 30 days' fast of Ramaḍān, General Kaufman answered that he could not satisfy their request, because cannons served a different purpose and had nothing to do whatsoever with the religious rites of the natives. The natives then had the idea to stress that they were the tsar's loyal subjects for whose long life they prayed in the mosques ... In his answer, the general pointed out to them that praying for the tsar and his long life was praiseworthy, because his imperial decrees aimed at promoting the well-being of his subjects – the Turkestan natives, who largely profited from the internal peace now brought to Turkestan (6a), from safety and the inviolability which now protected religion, family and social life, all of which also contributed to the material improvement of the natives. But, the general added, if the natives did not pray for our common sovereign, he would not force them to do so, because the Russian sovereign had many million coreligionists praying for him all over Russia... After this incident the natives did not renew their request to allow the use of the tsarist cannons on their main Islamic holiday, and general Kaufman did not insist on their praying for the tsar in the mosques in return, leaving it to their personal judgment. My arrival in Tashkent at the end of August 1877 coincided with the beginning of the Islamic fast,[185] sometime in early September. The first week I visited the general reporting on the school department the day before Friday (Thursday evening) and he never mentioned to me that the Muslims of Tashkent held a public prayer for the Russian Sovereign on Fridays. Neither did I hear anything on this matter when I was serving under generals Kolpakovskii,[186] Abramov[187] and Cherniaev[188] in business matters. But in 1888, during

---

[185] In 1877 the Islamic fast started on September 9.

[186] Kolpakovskii – G. A. Kolpakovskii (died in 1896) – general of the infantry and military governor of Semirech'e district. In 1881-1882 he replaced the sickly K. P. fon Kaufman, who had been the first Turkestan governor-general (Semenov, 1910, III-LII).

[187] Abramov – A. K. Abramov (died in 1886), lieutenant-general, hero of the Turkestan campaigns, twice Georgian knight. In 1868 he was established as the first military governor in Samarkand (Semenov, 1910, XXVI-XXVII).

[188] Cherniaev – M. G. Cherniaev (1828-1898) was lieutenant-general of the Russian army. He lead the Russian occupation of Tashkent (1865). He was military governor of the Turkestan krai (1865-1866) and governor-general of the Turkestan krai (1882-1884) (see: MacKenzie, 1974). – In this connection, it is not without interest to report what Muḥammad Ṣāliḥ Tāshkandī (born in 1830; about him see: A. Urinbaev, O. Buriev. *Toshkent Mukhammad Solikh tavsifida.* Toshkent, 1983; Sh. Vokhidov, *XIX asr Toshkent tarikhchilari.* Toshkent, 1996) has to say in his *"Tā'rīkh-i jadida-i Tāshkand"* (written 1863-1888). In this important source, we read that general Cherniaev convocated a meeting of the ulama of Tashkent in the Khoja Aḥrār mosque. The meeting took place on the first day of the new Islamic year – 1st *muḥarram* 1300/Sunday, November 12, 1882. And apparently, Cherniaev obliged them to control the observance of the Sharia and costumary laws by the local population of Tashkent. From the regrets and other comments by

the author and the participants of the meeting it becomes clear, that under pressure from the general, already at that time rules on the spiritual guidance of the local population were established that pleased the colonial authorities, and that these rules also concerned the regulation of religious rituals (the Persian original is published in Appendix 3.4):

"On the first of Muḥarram 1300 which was a year of the sheep Governor Cherniaev let the notables of Tashkent, the descendants of the Prophet, the Muslim scholars and other honorable men come to the Khoja Aḥrār Valī mosque in Tashkent and the common people, high and low, as well. On that occasion, an election from among the noble and learned men of the four quarters which make up the city of Tashkent was made, three excellent scholars from each quarter were chosen. First, from the Shaikhāwand-Ṭahūr quarter: the select of this time, the ocean of learning in our period, Īshān Sharīf Khoja Qāḍī, the brilliant son of Īshān Pādishāh Khoja Zībāchī, and Mullā Abū l-Qāsim Khalīfa, and Mullā Minhāj Qārī. Second, from the Besh Aghach quarter: the *sajda-nishīn* of our time, Abū l-Qāsim Khān Īshān, and Īshān ʿĀdil Khoja, and Mullā Aʿẓam Qāḍī. Third, from the Kūkcha quarter: Mullā Bāymīrzā Ākhūnd, and Dāmullā Hādī Aʿlam, and Mullā Ṣāliḥ Ākhūnd Khalīfa. Fourth, from the Sībzāriyān quarter: Mullā ʿAzīzlār Khān Aʿlam, and Mullā ʿAbd ar-Rasūl Aʿlam, and Ārtūq Khoja Ḥājjī Khalīfa. Then, the entirety of the legal affairs to which the rules of the sharia of the Prophet [eulogy] apply, with all their details, were conferred on to this group of scholars from Tashkent, and they were also entrusted with the legal affairs under customary law, and the drawing up of all legal documents (purchase deeds and the like) was committed to these outstanding scholars and adornments of our day. During this commotion which recalled the Day of Judgment, and in this most sacred musk-scented house of worship, the most excellent and knowledgeable jurist, the most select scholar in jurisprudence of our time and day, Dāmullā Hādī Aʿlam, the most learned of the learned, spoke to this most unworthy student and uttered the following speech: "O you who are binding together like a bookbinder the scattered events, o you who are selecting the script for the genealogy of the rulers: It is for the well-being of the two brilliant stars in Gemini that the Establisher of the Islamic faith(s) and the notable people and the Muḥammadan nations [eulogy] has set up three signs. The first sign is that today is the first day of the week, the second that today is the first day of Muḥarram and thus the beginning of (writing down the events of) a New Year, and the third is that we are writing 1300 the same day general Rozenbakh's term of office, for the first time the city major of Tashkent, Colonel Putintsev,[189] approached me with the general's order to examine the anthology "Khutbalyk", well-known in Kazan, in which the Friday

---

when the Russians have become 300 [?] [or: when three men each have become heads?]. Furthermore, the weighty matter of establishing the Religion of Aḥmad [Muḥammad] has been completed today, and in future, the sealing of those matters will proceed and progress from day to day, and so on until the very end [the end of Time]. There are not many months and years in the past and in the future which have been gifted with such a result and such an outcoming, and not often has the renewal of the people in the world been so effective. Haven't you heard that new things are always delicious?""

(Translator's comment: The "native town" of Tashkent was divided into four quarters, the Russian town was added.

*A'lam* is a title for people who are giving legal response (Bukharan usage).

*sajda-nishīn,* "who is sitting on the prayer rug", is used for the acting head of a Sufi brotherhood.

*īshān* is used for dignified people generally, and for members of Sufi brotherhoods in particular.

Other titles also point to the distinction the enumerated persons have in the Islamic sciences.

The "two brilliant stars in Gemini", Castor and Pollux in western languages, are called *at-tu'ām ash-sharqī* and *at-tu'ām al-gharbī* in Arabic, the "eastern twin" and the "western twin". In rhetoric style, these expressions can be used as a metaphor for the East and the West.

I have not been able to find a solution to the "300 Russians". The text may be corrupt and a conjecture would yield the proposed alternative.

In the last paragraph, the author alludes to the concept of *tajdīd,* "renewal"; a renewer is expected for every century. – End of translator's note to the translation from Persian. Translation from the Persian and notes: Jürgen Paul.)

(Muḥammad b. Ṣāliḥ, Ta'rīkh-i jadīda-i Tāshkand, OIRUz-1, Nr. 11072/2, 162b-164a).

See Ostroumov's essay on Muslim loyalty to the Russian presence and on native prayers in the mosques "for the wealth" of the Russian tsar during the time of governor-general K. P. fon Kaufman.

[189] Putintsev – S. R. Putintsev – colonel of artillery, captain of the city of Tashkent (1883-1892).

sermons (*khuṭbas*) read at the end of Friday worship among the Kazan Tatars were collected in print (6b). In these *khuṭbas* monotheism is praised and Gods mercy is asked for the prophet Muḥammad and his family, and after that, in addition, for the ruling sovereign (*pādishāh*), and it is added to which particular ruling sovereign the prayer is related: maybe the Turkish sultan or the former khan of the Golden Horde, since this was also common practice of Uzbek khan.[190] The reason for this order to examine the "Khutbalyk" was unusual: General Rozenbakh planned to celebrate the upcoming name-day of his wife Ol'ga Ivanovna (July 11, 1888) with two festivities – the new consecration of the now finished military cathedral and a special ceremony in the native town on occasion of the handing over to the native population of the Khoja Aḥrār Friday mosque which had been rebuilt with tsarist funding. Merging these two ceremonies was a large and spiritual idea – the bringing together of two religious cults as a proof for the religious tolerance of the Russian government in Turkestan. The bishop of Vernyi,[191] Neofit,[192] came to Tashkent for the consecration of the cathedral, but for the handing over of the reconstructed mosque they had thought of a special ceremony which was to feature the reading of a prayer for the tsar and the setting up of the tsar's portrait in the mosque. The booklet "Khutbalyk" had been freshened up with carmine red velvet. The text of the prayer itself had been rearranged to include the name of the sovereign and the crown prince. But the plan of the merging of two

[190] Uzbek khan – ruler of the Golden Horde (1312-1342). He turned Islam into state religion in his realm.
[191] Vernyi – name of the city of Alma-ata/Almaty until 1921.
[192] Neofit – Neofit (Nevodchikov) –orthodox clergyman, from 1883-1892 he was the third bishop in Tashkent and Turkestan.

religious ceremonies on the occasion of his wife's name-day in the form that the governor-general had invented was not to materialize: on July 11, bishop Neofit did consecrate the military cathedral, but the consecration of the reconstructed mosque in the native town was postponed for reasons unknown to me, perhaps they simply had not finished, maybe because of gossiping jokers. (7a) The so called consecration of the Khoja Aḥrār mosque was finally carried out on July 29, but, for reasons unknown to me, in a not actually ceremonial frame. The official description of this event (issue 33 of "*Turkestanskie vedomosti*"), however, adapted the event so that it fitted the Kazan model. After that, general Rozenbakh never again mentioned the failed attempt to unite two completely different events – one of them orthodox-ecclesiastical and the other one simply administrative, having nothing whatsoever in common with Islamic cults (***It is enough to recall that the imam of the Khoja Aḥrār mosque was instructed to play a role so unfamiliar to him, reading a prayer for an unbelieving ruler, and that when the deputy imam read the Kazan khuṭba, he perspired so much and so distorted the names of the sovereign and the crown prince when he pronounced them that even general Rozenbakh couldn't help smiling. All this was so singular and so funny that there is no need to even discuss other decrees from the Russian government concerning prayers for the tsar as correspondent D. hypothesizes... The following cholera-revolt*[193] *in Tashkent in 1892 and the assault of the*

[193] The cholera revolt – a rebellion, that took place on June 14, 1892, during the time of the cholera epidemic in Tashkent. Reasons given for the rebellion were the measures taken by the local administration against the further spreading of the epidemic. Those measures were taken without any explanation (they consisted, e.g., in closing all the

*Ferghana Muslims on the Russian military camp in 1898 show that the natives of Turkestan do not have any sympathy at all with the prayer for the tsar and for the tsarist government; that is not surprising, but conforms with the teaching of the Quran, Surah 4, verse ... ).* General Rozenbakh never wanted to be informed either about whether or not the *khuṭba* for the Russian sovereign and the ruling house of Russia was read on Fridays in the mosques of Tashkent.

This continued until 1892, when someone reminded baron Vrevskii of the prayer for the Russian tsar, the new text, which had been elaborated, but so clumsily, by an assembly of cadis[194] in Tashkent and had been approved by the baron already in a renewed version, as was mentioned above. In this second redaction, the prayer (7b) for the Russian tsar and the Russian ruling house was not read in the Muslim madrasas and mosques, but in the Russo-native schools, and it didn't have any influence on Muslim opinion at all. The mullahs, studying in the madrasas, did not think themselves obliged to even remember the names of the ruling family in Russia. However, the "Last word" which the sheikh of Baghdad[195] addressed to Europe showed that the

---

existing cemeteries), which caused the population to protest. (*Tashkent. Entsiklopedia.* Tashkent, 1984, 72).

[194] In agreement with the "Administrative situation of the Turkestan region" (part 2, chapter III, §§230, 237, 241, 243, 244-251) important verdicts concerning Muslims were supposed to be taken by a council of judges or special councils of judges, but not by single national judges (cadis).

[195] I.e. the work of 'Abd al-Ḥaqq, "*Poslednee slovo islama Evrope*", published at the end of the 19th century. Ostroumov quoted this work many times in his well known book "*Koran i progress*" (Ostroumov, 1901, 200-203, 245). In this book Ostroumov sees 'Abd al-Ḥaqq as a pan-Islamic author (24, 203, 211). See one of the editions of mentioned

Christian nations do not have any basis to hope for enduring friendly relations to be established with the Muslims. The national self-confidence of the Muslims of Russia and Turkestan which awoke with the 1917 revolution did not satisfy itself with the formation of federal republics. Instead, it pushed progressive Muslims to the secret organization of pan-Turkist[196] and pan-Islamist[197] governments, as appears from reports about the political trial of Kasymov[198] in Central Asia and Sultan-Galiev[199] in inner Russia (in Bashkiria). In the light of the circumstances just explained, I quite naturally came to the conclusion that the very idea of Muslims praying for an unbelieving tsar and powers is not congenial to Muslims, and was indeed preached by Saint

---

book: Shaikh ʿAbd al-Ḥaqq Baghdādī, *Falāḥa doğru; Islamīyetin Avrupaya son sözü* (translator:) Shaikh Muḥsin-i Fānī. Der Seʿādet, 1331 (1914) ("Towards Salvation. Islam's Last Word to Europe").

[196] Pan-Turkism – a movement that arose with the goal of uniting all Turkish nations. It developed in Turkey at the end of the 19th – beginning of the 20th century.

[197] Pan-Islamism - a movement that arose in Islamic countries during the 19th century. After the October revolution in 1917 it became the ideological weapon of Central Asian Muslims against Soviet power, one part of the opposition (on those two movements see: Khalid, 2000, 194-198).

[198] The Kasymov trial – a campaign which the Soviet government conducted in 1929-1930 with the aim of accusing and intimidating the local intelligentsia inTurkestan. Head of the "Kasymovs", allegedly, was Sa"dulla Kasymov, president of the High Court of the Uzbek SSR. In 1929 he was arrested and accused of having attempted to organize a nationalist party. Along with him many other high functionaries of the Uzbek SSR were charged. Due to these trumped-up accusations, they all were shot as enemies of the state (*Uzbekistonning yangi tarikhi*, 2000, 322).

[199] The trial of Sultan-Galiev – an analogous campaign against the Tatar leader Sultangaliev Mirsaid and his followers, as a result of which mass repressions began during the 1930ies in the Soviet Union (Khalid, 2000, 193; Rzehak, 2001, 304).

Paul[200] in the following verses: (8a) "*First of all, then, I urge that supplications, prayers, intercessions, and thanksgivings be made for all men, for kings and all who are in high positions, that we may lead a quiet and peaceable life, godly and respectful in every way. This is good, and it is acceptable in the sight of God our Savior,*" (First letter of Paul to Timothy, chapter 2, verse 1-4).[201] Jesus: "*Let every person be subject to the governing authorities. For there is no authority except from God, and those that exist have been instituted by God. Therefore he who resists the authorities resists what God has appointed, and those who resist will incur judgment.*" (Letter of Paul to the Romans, chapter 13, verse 1-2).[202] Christ's prescription to the apostles enjoining them to obey the powerful and to pray for them spread all over the world and was widely accepted by non-Muslim nations as soon as they came into contact with Christians. Regarding the natives of Central Asia it could be interesting to note that the Christian tradition to pray for the powers in place was known to Chingis Khan[203] and his descendants. As V.V. Bartol'd notes in his article "The history of the Turko-Mongol peoples" (Tashkent, 1928, page 16),[204] Christianity was widespread in Mongolia in the 13$^{th}$ century, with perhaps Uyghur influence behind that. Bartol'd's theory is supported by a note in the "Yasa"[205] or "Yasak", the legal collection

---

[200] Saint Paul – one of the apostles in Christianity. According to the church, the "New Testament" contains his 14 books.

[201] See *The Holy Bible. First letter of Paul to Timothy.*

[202] See *The Holy Bible. Letter of Paul to the Romans.*

[203] Chingis Khan (1155-1227) – founder and great khan of the Mongol empire (1206-1227).

[204] V.V. Bartol'd, *Sochinenia.* Vol. V. Moskva, 1968, 205ff.

[205] The anthology of laws/legislation were announced when Chingis Khan was chosen/elected as ruler (1206). The texts have come down to

made on behalf of Chingis Khan pointing to the tradition of the Christian clergy praying for the tsar (8b).

In a decree of Chingis Khan, dated 1223 and issued for the head of the Tibetan religious teaching, we read: "A holy order from tsar Chingis, an order for the chiefs of all places. Whatever there is of hermitages and houses of asceticism under the order of Tsyushen-syan, let their inmates who are daily reading holy books and praying to heaven, pray for the tsar's life to last for many years" ...[206]

In 1270, the khan Mengu-Temur[207] wrote in his decree to the Rus',[208] meant for the clerics: "Everything ... belongs to God they themselves also belong to God. Let them pray for us."

The khan Berke,[209] brother of Baty,[210] destined the yearly tribute gathered in the whole district of Rostov to the cathedral of Rostov and its metropolite Kirill[211] and in return ordered that in all Rostov prayers be chanted for the health of the khan's son who really recovered.

---

us in fragments. - This is surrounded by a certain controversy; see the summary in Reuven Amitai-Preiss: *The Mongol Empire and its Legacy*. Leiden 1999. Translators' addition.

206 Unfortunately, I wasn't able to identify the source the quoted passage was taken from.

207 Mengu-Temur – ruler of the Golden Horde (1266-1280).

208 The old name for Russia.

209 Khan Berke – ruler of the Golden Horde (1257-1266), the younger brother of Baty. - It is Berke who is credited with the first islamizing policy in the Golden Horde. See Jean Richard, "Berke et la conversion de la Horde d'or", *Revue des Etudes Islamiques* 35 (1967), 173-184; and Devin DeWeese, *Islamization and Native Religion in the Golden Horde*. University Park (Pennsylvania), 1994. Translators' addition.

210 Baty – (Batu) ruler of the Golden Horde (1243-1255), grandson of Chingis Khan.

211 Kirill – metropolit, lived during the 13th century.

Because of the prayers of the Moscovite metropolite Aleksii[212] the Khan'ena ... (Taydula, the wife of Janibek-khan[213], son of Uzbek-khan) was healed from a lethal disease and for this she took under her protection many Russians (***See doctor Elenzhen Khara-davan's book "Chingis-khan as army commander and his heritage", Belgrade, 1929, p. 213-214*). (9a)

In "Collected materials for the history of the Golden Horde", edited by V. Tizengauzen in 1884 in St. Petersburg, there are references to prayers for ruling Muslim caliphs, sultans and khans. For instance, in his chronicle, the secretary of the Egyptian sultan Baybars, [214] the cadi Ibn ʿAbd al-Ẓāhir[215] (d. 1293 AD) relates that sultan Baybars liked khan Berke, the Mongol khan of the Golden Horde, and prayed for his victory over his enemies (page 57). The Abbasid[216] caliph Al-Ḥākim bi-amrillāh[217] read a prayer for the sultan of Egypt and for the khan of the Horde, Berke, on Friday, June 7, 1263 (AD) (page 58). The Egyptian sultan wrote that prayers would be read for the khan in Mekka, Medina and Jerusalem when khan Berke's envoy would come to the

---

[212] Aleksii (died in 1378) – a Russian metropolit from 1354 on. A great politician of his epoch (see: B. D. Grekov, A. Yu. Yakubovskii, *Zolotaia orda i ee padenie.* Moskva, 1950, 120, 222, 239).

[213] Janibek (died in 1357) – khan of the Golden Horde (from 1342).

[214] Sultan Baybars – al-Malik al-Ẓāhir Rukn al-Dīn Baybars al-Bunduqdārī (1260-1277). A Mamluk ruler, famous under the name Sultan Baybars ( EI², I, 1158).

[215] Ibn ʿAbd al-Ẓāhir - Muḥyī al-Dīn Abu l-Faḍl ʿAbdallāh b. ʿAbd al-Ẓāhir. He wrote the chronicle "*Sīrat al-malik al-Ẓāhir*" ("*Zhizne-opisanie al-Malik al-Zahira*") (Tizengauzen, 1884, 46).

[216] The Abbasids – a dynasty of Arab caliphs (750-1258).

[217] Al-Ḥākim bi-amrillāh – one of the Abbasid caliphs, lived during the 13th century. - He was one of the puppet Abbasids kept at Cairo for the convenience of the emerging Mamluk sultans; his name was Aḥmad b. al-Ḥasan; he reigned from 1262-1302. - Translators' addition.

holy cities and that in the invocations[218] (khuṭba?) Berke would be mentioned after the sultan (page 61-62). In his chronicle, El-Mufaḍḍal[219] mentions that all over the realm of Uzbek-khan (one of Berke's descendants) prayers were recited from the minbars[220] for the Egyptian sultan al-Malik an-Nāṣir[221] after the prayer for he Tatar ruler Uzbek-khan (page 198). In his chronicle, Ibn Baṭṭūṭa[222] (d. 1347 AD) narrates that when he visited the Emir of Azov,[223] after refreshments had been served, a reciter gave a sermon in high-style Arabic about those who prayed for Uzbek-khan,[224] for the Emir of Azov and for all those present (page 285). But nowhere in the published chronicles of the Arabic travelers who had been to the lands of the Golden Horde, a prayer of the

[218] Invocation - part of the orthodox church service. The expression *ekteniya* comes from the Greek, "eagerness" being the basic meaning. The meaning *khuṭba* is in fact confirmed by the Arab original as published by Tizengauzen. Translators' addition.

[219] Al-Mufaḍḍal - Al-Mufaḍḍal b. Abī l-Faḍā'il, an Arab writer and author of chronicles. Tizengauzen in his book quotes a fragment of his work, where he describes the events of 1259-1341 concerning the Golden Horde (Tizengauzen, 1884, 176; EI², VII, 307).

[220] Pulpit – here, the *minbar*.

[221] Sultan al-Malik al-Nāṣir: Muḥammad b. Qalawūn Nāṣir ad-Dīn, Mamluk sultan. Contemporary of Uzbek Khan. Third reign: 703/1310-741/1341. - The relationships between the Mamluk sultans in Egypt and the khans of the Golden Horde in the southeastern European steppes were friendly most of the time (because they had common enemies, and because the Egyptian rulers relied on the steppe regions for their supply in young slaves), and this friendship was, as Ostroumov stresses, also expressed by having *khuṭbas* said for mutual benefit. - Translators' addition.

[222] Ibn Baṭṭūṭa (1304-1377): famous Arab traveler and author of a equally famous travelogue (See: N. Ibragimov, *Ibn Battuta i ego puteshestviia po Srednei Azii.* Moskva, 1988).

[223] The Emir of Azov - Muḥammad Khoja al-Khorazmī, ruled for the khans the Golden Horde in the area of Azov.

[224] This took place in 1333.

Muslims for the princes of Moscow[225] is mentioned. (9b) And consequently, there is no foundation at all to presume that the Kazan, Astrakhan and Crimean Tatars, after they had been conquered by the Russian unbelievers, prayed for their conquerors because they were unbelievers whilst in the Quran no prayers in favor of unbelievers are mentioned.

## *Text 3.2*

## First *khuṭba*[226]
## Translation

### Prayer for His Imperial Majesty

1. Oh Lord, save and preserve his Majesty the great emperor, our Alexander Alexandrovitch, his spouse, the

---

[225] The princes of Moscow – the rulers of the great principality of Moscow. The concerned principality was the Russian state established during the middle of the 14th century (*Moskva.Entsiklopediia*. Moskva, 1980, 429). - That no *khuṭba* was said in favor of the Moscovite princes does not show so much that no such prayers were ever said for unbelievers, but rather that the Moscow princes were considered as vassals, not sovereigns; for that reason, having a *khuṭba* read even for Muslim princes in the region would have been out of the question. As far as the Mongols are concerned, a general respect for everybody and every cult which might have some contact to supernatural powers has often been noted. See Donald Ostrowski: *Muscovy and the Mongols. Cross-cultural influences on the steppe frontier, 1304-1589.* Cambridge 1998. - Translators' addition.

[226] The original of the text is in the TsGARUz, I-1009, opis' 1, delo 34, fol. 19. I translated the text into Russian and numbered the lines throughout.

Empress Maria Fedorovna and his great Imperial Highness, the crown prince – Tsesarevich Nicolai Alexandrovich and protect the entire Imperial house for many years with kindness. Give these protectors of the world good health and provide these lords with wealth in all their affairs.

2. Bless, Lord, the ruling majesty, our Emperor, help this protector of the world to defeat the enemies of the Russian state and sow fear in the hearts of the evildoers, to help him show mercy to the righteous to support the poor and the destitute, to be a father to all his subjects who rejoices in their well-being.

3. Lord, give all of us health and a peaceful mind under the rule of our Majesty the Emperor, give us clean air and water in abundance, soothing rain and good harvests and blessing for us in both worlds.

Amen, oh God, Lord of the world!

This prayer must be recited in all Islamic *masjids* of Turkestan province on all Imperial holidays in complience with the order of his Excellency, the Lord governor-general of Turkestan, Baron Vrevskii.

## *Text 3.3*

Second *khuṭba*[227]
Translation

PRAYER FOR THE SOVEREIGN

227 TVG, 25.11.1894, Nr. 43. The newspaper printed the text of the *khuṭba* in Uzbek with the present Russian translation.

1. Save, Lord, and preserve our SOVEREIGN THE EMPEROR, NICOLAI ALEXANDROVICH, HER MAJESTY THE EMPRESS ALEXANDRA FEODOROVNA; MOTHER OF HIS HIGHNESS THE EMPRESS MARIA FEODOROVNA; THE CROWN PRINCE TSESAREVICH the Great Prince GEORGY ALEXANDROVICH and the whole Most Noble House for many years. Give THEM health and salvation, wealth and splendid prosperity in all THEIR affairs.
2. Bestow, Lord, upon on the ruling MAJESTY, our EMPEROR your blessing, help this protector of the world to defeat the enemies of the Russian state and to frighten the wrong-doers and to show mercy on the righteous, to support the poor and the destitute, to be a FATHER to all his subjects, who rejoices in their well-being.
3. Give, God, all of us health and a peaceful mind under the rule of our MAJESTY the EMPEROR, give us clean air, water in abundance, blessed rain, good harvests and abundance in both worlds. Amen.

This prayer is being printed in the newspaper on the order of His Excellency, the Lord Governor-General of Turkestan, to be read in the mosques of Turkestan province and the Russo-native schools on all imperial holidays.

The above mentioned imperial holidays are the following: April 23, May 4 and 25, July 22, October 21, and November 14 and 26, December 6.[228]

---

[228] The holidays are the tsarist days, see above in the essay of Ostroumov.

# Appendix

## *Texts*

### *Text 1:*
### *Lyrical* munājāt *on the conquest of Khiva*

بسم الله الرحمن الرحيم

كافر بزبد لعنتى نينك بيان    اورص كيلكانينى بيانى تورور

| | | |
|---|---|---|
| 1. | قادير ايكام كرشمانكدين ايلاناى | اوز قدر اتينک بيلان يوق ايت كافرنى |
| 2. | بنده ميز عاجزميز نه علاج قيلاى | اوز قدر اتينک بيلان يوق ايت كافرنى |
| 3. | قدر اتينک يتمايمو حضرت پهلوان | قلعهُ يابان نى ايتب دور حيران |
| 4. | مسلمانلار يغلار بغريمز بر يان | اوز قدر اتينک بيلان دفع قيل كافرنى |
| 5. | هر مسجدا قوينغه ساليبدور اوتون | آلهى قالمسون بريسى بوتون |
| 6. | مسلمانلار غه ضرر يتمسدين بورون | اوز قدر اتينک بيلان يوق ايت كافرنى |
| 7. | فعلى ميز بورولدى چكدوک جزاميز | اكر اولمساک آرمان بيله بارامیز |
| 8. | نوح پيغمبر سينكا كوب دور ثناميز | اوز قدر اتينک بيلان يوق ايت كافرنى |
| 9. | قيغودين اولوب ميز كيچهُ كوندوز | آلهى كافرنى يوق ايتكاى سن تيز |
| 10. | آدينكدين آيلاناى قونكشيم يا | يغلاتمه مؤمين لارنى يوق ايت |

| | | |
|---|---|---|
| | قرق قیز | کافرنی |
| 11. | کافر کیلدی قلعمیزده آتوشدی | مسلمانلار یغلاب حقغه یاپوشدی |
| 12. | آمیرمیز نیتسون باریب یاراشدی | اوز قدراتینک بیلان یوق ایت کافرنی |
| 13. | بوزوب کیردی یانکی قلعه بندیدین | مدد ایستعانت تیلارمن سندین |
| 14. | آدینکدین آیلانای یا سید علاوددین | اوز قدراتینک بیلان دفع قیل کافرنی |
| 15. | آریک نی آلدیندا اویناتدی سرباز | یراتغان ایکام دین کیلکای بر آواز |
| 16. | آتینکدین ایلانای پیریم تورت شهباز | اوز قدراتینک بیلان یوق ایت کافرنی |
| 17. | کافر کیلیب چیقدی آق شیخ اوستینه | آریک نینک ایچینه کیردی دستینه |
| 18. | حضرت علی پریم کیلینک آنینک قصدینه | اوز قدراتینک بیلان یوق ایت کافرنی |
| 19. | بیش آلتی سی کیلیب چقدی مناره | مسلمان بنده نی قیلدی آواره |
| 20. | مناجات آیلارام حق پرواره | اوز قدرتینک بیلان دفع ایت کافرنی |
| 21. | حضرت پهلوان قایتیب آلغای طوفینی | کافره قراتیب آتغای اوقینی |
| 22. | بیلمادوک پهلوانی باری یوقینی | اوز قدراتینک بیلان یوق ایت کافرنی |
| 23. | دوغمه سیز جوری سیز زار اولماس | ایکام دولت بیرسا خوار زار اولماس |
| 24. | کیتکان دوغمه جوریلار یولی اولماس | یغلاتمه مؤمین نی یوق ایت کافرنی |
| 25. | خان حضرتمیز چقدیلار قلعه دین دیشان | امیرمیز یغلاب بولدی پریشان |
| 26. | بر مدد ایلای کور قیرجان ایشان | مدد بیریب تیزراق یوق ایت کافرنی |
| 27. | خان حضرتیمیز کییب دور کوهنه لباسی | یادیندین چقیب دور کیمخاسی تاسی |
| 28. | آلهی یار بولغای اتا باباسی | اوز قدراتینک بیلان یوق ایت کافرنی |
| 29. | خان حضرتیمز نی مینکان | کافر کیریب خزینه نی داله دی |

| | | |
|---|---|---|
| | اطی آله دور | |
| 30. | آریک نی ایچیندا بر ذات قالمدی | انصاف ایت خدایم یوق ایت کافرنی |
| 31. | خان حضرتیمز قوش چکیب چیقتی قلادین | مسلمانلارنی حق ساقلادی بلادین |
| 32. | شام سحر تیلاکیم شول الله دین | رحم ایت مسلمانلارغه یوق ایت کافرنی |
| 33. | خان حضرت میزنی رحم ایتکای سن تختینه | اولیالار کیلکان بولغای بختینه |
| 34. | کافر قورسون قراب بولماس سختینه | اوز قدراتینک بیلان یوق ایت کافرنی |
| 35. | یورتیمز اورکوشتی کافر کیلدی دیب | چاپدی مانکغیت لینی مالین آلدی دیب |
| 36. | توقوز یوز مسلمان شهید بولدی دیب | اوز قدراتینک بیلان یوق ایت کافرنی |
| 37. | رحم ایتکای سن خان حضرتنی یاشینه | کافر قاشوق سالدی ایچان آشینه |
| 38. | ینه دولت قوشی قونغای آنینک باشینه | اوز قدراتینک بیلان یوق ایت کافرنی |
| 39. | حضرت پهلوان قایتیب کیرکای قبرینه | کافرنینک نظری توشتی طوفینه |
| 40. | اوز قدراتینک بیلان دفع قیل کافرنی | آدینکدین آیلانای یا عبدال بابا |
| 41. | اوز قدرتینک بیلان یوق ایت کافرنی | قایته باشدین ایکا بولغای یورتینه |
| 42. | اوز قوراتینک بیلان یوق ایت کافرنی | حضرت پهلوان قایتب کیرکای قلاغه |
| 43. | کافرنینک کله سین آتغای هواغه | مسلمانلار قورقوروب بارماس نمازه |
| 44. | اورس فریار دیوب توشتی اوازه | قشالار قانی دیب یغلار دروازه |
| 45. | اوز قدراتینک بیلان یوق ایت کافرنی | مسلمانلار قورقوب ایشکین ایلدی |
| 46. | خان حضرت نی یغلاب بغرینی تیلدی | عبد الله خان دیوب ایلده بیلیندی |
| 47. | اوز قدراتینک بیلان یوق ایت کافرنی | کافر کوچه لارده قویدوردی سالداد |
| 48. | کافرنینک آلنیدین داد ایله بیداد | کوچوب کیتی کورلان بیلان |

| | | غزابات |
|---|---|---|
| 49. | اوز قدراتینک بیلان یوق ایت کافرنی | زریکا شیطانه بیردی کوب آزارنی |
| 50. | معنی سی بولمادی ینه بازارنی | کافر کوچه لارده اوزاردی طناب |
| 51. | کافرنینک آلنیدین بولدی بغریمز کباب | الهی کافرنی قیلغای سن خراب |
| 52. | شاد ایت مسلمانینی یوق ایت کافرنی | خوارزمدا یاتغان سانسز اولیا |
| 53. | بنده لار کوزیاشی بولوبدور دریا | یورتغه دینجلیقینی برکیل قادیر الله |
| 54. | تیلاکیمیز اوزینک یوق ایت کافرنی | کافر قوروغای توشماسمز آنینک تلینه |
| 55. | تیز یراق یوق بولوب کیتکای ایلینه | آنده حضرت عزرائیل چیقغای یولینه |
| 56. | اوز قدراتینک بیلان یوق ایت کافرنی | اوزی کافر تیلی سوزلار فارسینی |
| 57. | قشاقلار قورقوب اورماس کوسینی | کافر آلدی خوارزمنی ایسینی |
| 58. | اوز قدراتینک بیلان یوق ایت کافرنی | ایشانلار قورقوبان ایتماس ذاکری |
| 59. | اوز قدراتینک بیلان یوق ایت کافرنی | کیسب آلدی نورمخدیم نی طنابین |
| 60. | بیزلارکا ایچوردی قیغو شرابین | قادر الله چولاق ایتکای سن بارین |
| 61. | اوز قدراتینک بیلان یوق ایت کافرنی | آتینک بابا ریسدور آصلینک پیغمبر |
| 62. | خان حضرتغه ینه بولغای سن رهبر | کولده چولده غایب یوران ایرانلار |
| 63. | اوز قدراتینک بیلان یوق ایت کافرنی | لشکر بغناب چیقتی آتاجان توره |
| 64. | مسلمانلار یغلاب ایتدی پره | اونک یانینده آمیر باباسی بیله |
| 65. | اوز قدراتینک بیلان دفع ایت کافرنی | سلطان ویس آنی آتغای دریاغه |
| 66. | مناجاتیم یتوشسون تیز الله غه | آدینک دین آیلنای ناریم جان بابا |
| 67. | اوز قدراتینک بیلان یوق ایت کافرنی | سندین مدد یا پریم حضرت پهلوان |
| 68. | کافرلارغه ینه سالغای سن قیران | سیزه کوماک بیرکای یا شاهمردان |

| | | |
|---|---|---|
| 69. | اوز قدراتینک بیلان یوق ایت کافرنی | کافر صورت باسار سیغینانی بت |
| 70. | آلهی کافرنی قیلغای سن نابود | آدینکدین ایلانای حضرت داود |
| 71. | اوز قدراتینک بیلان یوق ایت کافرنی | کافرلار جم بولوب کیردی قلاغه |
| 72. | کندیم کان چولیده قیلدیلار غوغا | یراتقان بیر و بار رحم ایت بنده کا |
| 73. | اوز قدراتینک بیلان یوق ایت کافرنی | حضرت پهلوانینی قیلیب دور صورت |
| 74. | همه قورقوب آنی ایتاردی زیارت | بیزلاره مشکل دور ایکام انصاف ایت |
| 75. | اوز قوراتینک بیلان یوق ایت کافرنی | حضرت پهلوان چراغ یاقمادی |
| 76. | حضرت پهلوان مسلمانه باقمادی | ایشینار قشاق قورقوب طبل قاقمادی |
| 77. | اوز قوراتینک بیلان یوق ایت کافرنی | بونه من من لیک دور خدا کوتارماس |
| 78. | صبر ایتب یتاندور پرلار کیچرماس | اوز قدراتینک بیلان یوق ایت کافرنی |
| 79. | خراب ایتدی آمیرمیزنی باغی | خان حضرت نی یوراکیدا کوب دور داغی |
| 80. | کافر مسلمانغه بولور مو یاغی | اوز قدراتینک بیلان یوق ایت کافرنی |
| 81. | تینمای یاد اینارمن شام سحرده | مسلمان کافره بولورمو بنده |
| 82. | ادینکدین آیلانای یا شاء زنده | اوز قدراتینک بیلان یوق ایت کافرنی |
| 83. | اوستونکدین یول بیردینک پریم نان یماس | یول سزنی خدادین اوزکاسی بیلماس |
| 84. | یازیمز قیش بولدی ای کون بیلماس | اوستونکدین یول بیردینک یوق ایت کافرنی |
| 85. | کافره اط قویدی چو دری یموت | بر مدد آیلا کور حضرت داود |
| 86. | همت آیستغانت پریم ایسماموت | اوز قدراتینک بیلان یوق ایت کافرنی |
| 87. | کافر قورسون قلامیزنی اوتلادی | خدایم یار بولدی اوزی ساقلادی |
| 88. | هیوه ستاننی پری قره الم بابادی | اوستونکدین یول بیردینک یوق ایت کافرنی |
| 89. | خانیمیز دولتی هم بولغای | یار بولغای خدایم محمد حبیب |

| | | |
|---|---|---|
| | نصیب | |
| 90. | دردلی نینک دردینه سن خاذق طبیب | اوز قدراتینک بیلان یوق ایت کافرنی |
| 91. | قوش بیکنی اوزی آمان سقلاسون | بارغان یرده دایم کل لار آچلسون |
| 92. | خدایم کافرنی خراب ایلاسون | بیر و باریم یوق ایت اوروس کافرنی |
| 93. | قوش بیکی بارغانده تیتراشور کافر | بارسه یزیدلاره توشادور غلغل |
| 94. | فقرا ایتادور خداغه شُکُر | ایرلار پرلار دف قیل کافرنی |
| 95. | قوش بیکی بارانده سلطنت بیله | کلفت نی یوق ایتیب خوشولیق قیله |
| 96. | کافرنینک اعضاسی تیتراشورینه | قادیر ایکام اوز ینک یوق ایت کافرنی |
| 97. | قوش بیکی آیتادور هرکز قورقمانکیز | کافرلارنینک ایچینه وهم سالورمیز |
| 98. | یزیدلار نی انشاءالله قیرارمیز | اوز قدراتینک بیلان یوق قیل کافرنی |
| 99. | کافر ویران ایتدی کهنه قلانی | آمیرمیز یاد آیلادی ینه الله نی |
| 100. | الهی تیز کیلکای قایتیب دورانی | خدایم یوق ایت اوروص کافرنی |
| 101. | کیرای چیقدی هزارسب نی یوقلادی | کافر مسلمانه طوفین اوقلادی |
| 102. | اونی شول وقت خدا ساقلادی | همیشه یار بولوب یوق ایت کافرنی |
| 103. | ایرانلار جیم بولوب کیردی قلاغه | فعلیمزدین قالدوق مونچه بلاغه |
| 104. | زار یغلادیم پریم زارلیق باباغه | خداغه یالباریب یوق ایت کافرنی |
| 105. | آدینکدین ایلانای یا حضر الیاس | سزیقین بنده سی دفع ایت کافرنی |
| 106. | دیوان بیکی نینک ادی محمد مرات | لشکرکا بُل بریب قیلمادی مُراد |
| 107. | یعقوب بای محمود نیاز قایتدیلار قونکرات | خدایم سن یوق ایت اورس کافرنی |
| 108. | ایرانلار باریب ایتکایلار خلاص | بلادین قوتولوب ایتکایمیز اخلاص |

اما عباد الله ایشانیمز نی بیرو توتوب آیدی یورت نینک فعل کیرداری یمانغه آیلاندی سز بزروک وارسیز بو ایشلارنی رخنه بیریب دفع قیلینک دیب ینه شول یرده بر سوز آیدیلار

| | | |
|---|---|---|
| 109. | قطب زمان ایکی جهان نینک پری | عالم نینک حالندین خبردار اولونک |
| 110. | کونکولونده بر زره قالمادی کیری | یورت نینک احوالیندین خبردار اولونک |
| 111. | سیزدین باشقه یوقتور قطب زمانی | بو ایّامده فرخی یوق یخشی یمانی |
| 112. | شفع کیلتوروب من قادیر الله نی | مریدلار حالیندین خبردار اولونک |
| 113. | اتا بابا‌ینکز ینه سلوک یوروتکان | راست قیا باقغانده تاغ نی ایرتکان |
| 114. | باطن کوزی بیله عرش نی سیر ایتکان | کاسیبلار حالیندین خبردار اولونک |
| 115. | زاهری فرشته بر قری کیشی | کیچه کوندوز ذکر ایتورسیز وورریشی |
| 116. | یراتغان الله غه یتار نالیشی | قلعه لار حالیندین خبردار اولونک |
| 117. | بزرک کیشی یورته چکار جیفانی | خدایم کورساتما ایمدی مونداغ بلانی |
| 118. | کافر کیلدی اوج ایلاندی قلانی | خداغه زار ایتب مددکار اولونک |
| 119. | کافر یوق بولوردی حق نی یاد ایتسا | یولدین چقغانلاردین خبردار اولونک |
| 120. | بنده لیک ایتمادی قادیر الله غه | پادشاه نینک حالیندین خبردار اولونک |
| 121. | آریک نینک مسجدی یاشیل تقشدی | کافر کیلیب یکرمه کون آتیشدی |
| 122. | فعلیمز یاقمادی ایرانلار قاشدی | ایمدی مسلمانه مددکار اولونک |
| 123. | سیز تانورسیز قیامت نی دفتری | بولاکورنک گمراهلارنینک رهبری |
| 124. | پادشاه بیلمادی خیر ایله شری | فقرا حالندین خبردار اولونک |
| 125. | تیلیمدا جاریدور ستارو جبار | ایمدی قالغان سیز دور صاحیب اختیار |
| 126. | اوزین آیتیب یغلار نسلی شیخ مختار | بارچه نینک حالندین خبردار اولونک |
| 127. | حق ایلچی سی اول جبرائیل | ملا ینکز خذمتکاریندە کمین |

128. پیغمبر مله کی دین خوارزمین دی آمین دی | خوارزمی حالندین خبردار اولونک دی

تمام بولدی لعنت کافر اوروس نینک سوزی قالغانلارغه اوزاق عمر پری پادشاهیمزنینک هم عُمری اوزاق بولوب صاحب خوروج بولغای آمین و یا رب العالمین
مینک ایکی یوز توقسان آلتی ده یازیلغان تمت ١٢٩٦
شد به توفیق خدا یا لا ینام این کتابت روز چهار شنبه تمام
یازغان کاتیب بیچاره نی دعا قیلیب یاد قیلغای سیز
منکه دعا طمعه دارم ذانکه من بنده کنه کارم
بو خط داملا قربان نیاز نکی تورور

## *Text 2:*

## *Lyrical* munājāt *with good wishes for the Russian emperor during the Russo-Japanese war*

یاپون ایلان روسسیه لارنی ارا سیده غی محاربه لاریغه اوش اویازیده اوش بولوستیده تاشلاق کذر دهه سیده تورغوچی ملا عمر اوزاق امام نظر اوغلی فقیرینی ایتکان اشعاریدور

1. یا رب سلامت ایتکیل عالم پناهمزنی
2. بزلارغه مهربان لیك اول دسكاهمزنی
3. برچه عالم نی تنچ قیلغان آكاهمزنی
4. هر آفتینکدین اسرا اول پادشاهمزنی
5. یتم بیوه بیچاره احوالیدین خبردار
6. کوب عدل دور عالمغه یزقدور ظلمیکه زینهار

7. آنی دشمنلاریغه یتکور بلانی بسیار
8. هر آفتینکدین اسرا بول پادشاهمزنی
9. قیلغان ایمش دریاده بیحد جنکی مغلوبین
10. محکم بیلینی باغلاب جناب کوراپاتکین
11. بول روسسیه عسکرلار آلماق قصدیده یاپون
12. هر آفتینکدین اسرا بول پادشاهمزنی
13. روسسیه لارغه یاری بیرغیل عسکرلاریغه
14. زیان زحمت نی یتکور یاپون لشکرلاریغه
15. بلانی برقی تیسون الم فکرلاریغه
16. هر آفتینکدین اسرا بول پادشاهمزنی
17. یاپونلارغه کورساتسون روسسیه ضربینی
18. یارب مبارك ایله فتح ایلاسون شهرینی
19. مدام دوران نی سورسون جهان بهرینی
20. هر آفتینکدین اسرا بول پادشاهمزنی
21. دایم دعاده دورلار اوشلیك برله اندجان
22. خلایقی مرغنان خوقند هم نمنکان
23. یارب قبول ایتکیل دیبان تابیع ترکستان
24. هر آفتینکدین اسرا بول پادشاهمزنی
25. زاره ایمدی الهیم روسسیه غه عنایت
26. قیلسه کرم موءمین لار دعاسی نی ایجابت
27. فقیری التماسین مقبول ایتسه دوامت
28. هر آفتینکدین اسرا بول پادشاهمزنی

هر وقت یازیب تورامیز کزیت، دیکان آینه مثل ایراك، هر خیل آدملارنینك حسن و قبحنی اوزیغه کورساتادور دیب اوش شهریدین یازیب یوبارکانی اوشبو شاعرنینك شعرینی بی تبدیل و بی تغیر کزیت که سالدوك تا کیم مذکور شعرنی ایچیده کی سجع و وزن و قافیه لاریده کی قبیح لارینی معاینه کورسه لار کیرك دیب اوتکان وقت لارده شونکا اوخشاش بر شاعرنینك شعری خصوصیده یازکان ایدوك * شعر ایتب سز همه بلند پس بریسی بر قریش بری اوچ کز دیب

## *Text 3.1*

### *Esssay by N.P. Ostroumov*

Остроумов Н. П.

История «молитвы за царя», предназначавшейся для чтения
в ташкентских мечетях и в русско-туземных школах
(***Настоящий очерк составлен в 1930 году, на основании записей в моем дневнике и нескольких изданий и статей, написанных в 20 столетии*)

Поводом к настоящему очерку послужили следующие факты:

В среду, 3 марта 1892 года, я прочитал в № 9 Туркестанских ведомостей заметку такого содержания: «Господин Главный начальник края (***барон Александр Борисович Вревский. - Н.О.*) изволили признать необходимым, чтобы в мусульманских мечетях Туркестанского края, в высокоторжественные дни: восшествия на престол Его Императорского Величества, в дни рождений Их Императорских Величеств и Государя Наследника, а также в день Нового года по мусульманскому летоисчислению, прихожанами возносились молитвы о здравии и долгоденствии Их Императорских Величеств и Государя Наследника – Цесаревича. Текст этой молитвы, выработанный съездом народных судей города Ташкента и утвержденный господином Главным Начальником Туркестанского края, следующий:

«Боже мой! Помоги, окажи милость Его Величеству Государю нашему Александру Александровичу с его супругой Великой Государыней Марией Федоровной и Наследнику(1[б]) Государю - Цесаревичу Николаю Александровичу и остальным августейшим Детям Его. Аминь.

Боже мой! Сделай царя всем Его подданным милостивым и дай царствовать Ему над нами постоянно. Аминь.

Боже мой! Сохрани царя и супругу Его с Августейшей семьей от бед небесных и земных, от зависти и покушений людских. Аминь.

Боже мой! Продли жизнь царя и дай Ему и роду Его вечно царствовать над нами. Аминь.

Боже мой! Да будут для нас дни Их рождений и вступления на престол священными. Аминь.

Боже мой! Сохрани также Его знатных министров, сподвижников преданных, верноподданных хранителей государства, и дай Ему постоянную победу над врагами. Аминь.

Боже мой! Да действуют выборные Его правители Его повелением. Аминь.

Боже мой! Да просвещаются под Его разумным правлением все: большие и малые, мужчины и женщины. Аминь». (2[a])

Меня заинтересовало это распоряжение барона Вревского, а некоторые выражения написанного текста молитвы вызвали недоумения, о которых я сообщил Главному инспектору училищ для доклада генерал-губернатору. Соглашаясь принципиально с основной идеей упомянутого распоряжения, я разъяснил Керенскому, что в Коране вообще не рекомендуется мусульманам доброжелательные и дружелюбные отношения к христианам (***«Верующие! Не берите в друзья себе ни иудеев, ни назарян» (христиан) глава 5, статья 56. И в другой главе Корана «Верующие не должны брать себе в друзья неверных, минуя верующих: а кто будет делать это, тому не будет защиты от Бога» (глава 3, статья 27, тоже в главе 4, статья 143). Эти и другие воззвания против неверных были высказаны Мохаммедом по отношению к его современникам; но позднее мусульмане ссылались на эти изречения, когда возникал вопрос об отношениях верующих к неверным, как это* *проявлялось в первые века ислама и после во времена столкновений мусульманских государей не только с христианскими, но и вообще с неверными, как указывалось в сборнике материалов В. Тизенгаузена, относящихся к истории Золотой Орды (С.-Петербург, 1884 г., том 1, стр. 98-следующие, и других известных арабских авторов, приводящихся в том же сборнике*) и что поэтому необходимо осторожнее относиться к религиозному чувству туземцев, покоренных оружием неверных и уже проявившим свое недовольство продолжением русского господства в Средней Азии, особенно после присоединения Ферганы к России (***Подразумевается вооруженное восстание ферганских туземцев на русский военный лагерь в Андижане в мае 1898 года. См. в брошюре П. Галузо «Туркестан – колония» (Москва, 1929 г.*). С этой же точки зрения я считал неубедительным принуждать туземцев к молитвенным воззваниям о вечном царствовании над ними русского царя и о постоянной победе его над врагами, в первом ряду которых стояли мусульманские соседние ханства в Средней Азии. Афганский хан Абдурахман пользовался поддержкой туркестанской(2[б]) администрации и клялся генералу Кауфману как претендент на афганский престол, а когда завладел Афганистаном, то никакого благожелательства к русским не обнаруживал (смотрите его записки в русском переводе полковника Грулева). В Коране запрещается мусульманам не только дружить с неверными и не любить их, хотя бы они (?...) родственниками (глава 58, статья 22), но предписывалось быть жестокими к ним, воевать с ними и избивать их беспощадно, чтобы не было соблазна для мусульман от неверных в единого Бога и потомка его Мохаммеда. В этом отношении заслуживает внимания два следующих изречения: «Господь наш! Не возлагай на нас того, что нам не по силам. Пощади нас, прости и помилуй нас. Ты – наш покровитель, даруй нам победу над народами неверующими (глава 2, статья 286). В другом изречении говорится: «Мы (последователи ислама) далеки от вас (неверных); между нами и вами великая вражда и ненависть навсегда, до той поры, пока вы не уверуете в Бога, который един» (глава 60, статья 4).

В виду приведенных изречений, я удивлен как могли официальные представители ислама, кадии ввести в текст молитвы за русского царя прошение о даровании ему постоянной победы над врагами… Оставаясь при своем сомнении в искренности сочиненной (кем?) молитвы за русского царя, я чувствую себя в неловком положении, потому что был обязан, по должности редактора(3[a]) туземной газеты перевести упомянутую молитву на местное наречие и напечатанный в газете перевод разослать в медресе и должностным туземцам через канцелярии уездных начальников. Таким образом, я становлюсь в невыгодном положении участника в распространении неудачного распоряжения главного начальника края относительно молитвы, содержание которой не выражает, по моему убеждению, действительных чувств туземцев. При этом я имел в виду неудачную попытку предшественника барона Вревского, генерал-губернатора Розенбаха прочитать молитву за царя по Казанскому сборнику (Хутбалык) в мечети Ходжи-Ахрара 29 июня 1888г. (***Поводом к этому послужила официальная передача генерала Розенбаха представителям туземного населения названной мечети после ее перестройки на деньги, пожертво-ванные государем Александром III-им через Бухарского Эмира по случаю коронации. Описание этой передачи было напечатано в «Туркестанских Ведомостях» (№ 33 от 23 августа 1888 года) в стиле казенного (правительственного) сообщения, не дающего действительной картины выдающегося события в жизни ташкентских туземцев*).

Сообщенные мной Керенскому сведения он доложил барону Вревскому, который согласился на изменение утвержденного им текста молитвы, одобренного кадиями. Керенский поручил мне составить другой текст молитвы, перевести измененный текст и, при одобрении его местными кадиями, представить на распоряжение генерала-губернатора.(3[б]) Составленный мной новый текст молитвы за царя был переведен при участии моего сотрудника по газете, бывшего кадия Саттархана Абдугафарова. Перевод был одобрен ташкентским кадием Мухиддином-ходжой 24 апреля 1892 г. (см. подробности в записях моего дневника). После этого молитва за царя и царствующий дом в новой редакции была напечатана и в отдельных оттисках разослана в туркестанские медресе, должностным туземцам в русско-туземные школы для чтения в соответствующие выходные и праздничные дни. Учащиеся в русско-туземных школах (сыновья ташкентских туземцев) заучили текст этой молитвы, как обыкновенную хрестоматийную статью, как и русский народный гимн, и читали ее хором (речитативом) при посещении школ русскими начальствующими лицами, особенно, на выпускных экзаменах, посещаемых генерал-губернатором, областным губернатором, начальником города, представителями учебных заведений и туземным населением и родителями учащихся. Но читалась ли эта молитва в мечетях в пятницу и в царские дни - я сомневаюсь, хотя представители туземцев на военных парадах в так называемые «царские дни» обыкновенно заявляли генерал-губернаторам, что в эти дни, (а именно говорили, что всегда) молитва читалась в мечетях за царя и царствующий дом (смотрите в записях моего дневника).

Казалось бы, что вопрос об установлении молитвы за царя исчерпан. Но нашим корреспондентом, прикрывшим свою личность буквой Д., была напечатана в № 109 газеты «Русская жизнь» от 23 апреля 1892 года заметка под заголовком «Молитва за царя в Туркестане» следующего содержания: (4[а])

«В №5780 «Нового времени» (1 апреля) сообщается, что туркестанский генерал-губернатор распорядился, чтобы в мечетях края, в высокоторжественные дни, а также в день Нового года, прихожане возносили молитвы о здравии Их Величеств и наследника Цесаревича. Газета прибавляет, что текст молитвы выработан съездом народных судей города Ташкента. Утвержден генерал-губернатором.

Сообщение это не совсем верно и требует поправки. Такое распоряжение сделано было еще в 1888 году и именно при следующих обстоятельствах. Во время коронации (1883 год) эмир Бухарский поднес Государю Императору подарок в 30000 рублей бухарскою монетою. Государю было благоугодно приказать употребить эти деньги на нужды Туркестанского края – и, во исполнение сей Монаршей воли местная власть распорядилась обратить эту сумму на возобновление некоторых особенно почитаемых мечетей. Таким обра-зом была возобновлена единственная по своей величественности мечеть Султан-Азрет в городе Туркестане, - затем починены старинная мечеть в селе Зангиата (15 верст от Ташкента) и заново перестроена мечеть Ходжа Ахрар в Ташкенте. После перестройки последняя мечеть получила в народе название «Царской». 29 июля 1888 года – бывший туркестанский генерал-губернатор Розенбах, при несколько торжест-венной обстановке передал эту мечеть муллам и кадиям и того же числа была произнесена в мечети молитва за царя, Наследника и весь Царствующий Дом. Насколько мне известно, молитва это не была никем сочинена, а форма ее оказалась в законе и потребовалось только перевести ее с казанского татарского наречия на сартовский язык. Затем молитва эта произносилась каждый мусульманский праздник (пятница).

Может быть, распоряжение о том, чтобы в мечетях молились за Царя, было делом и ранее 1888 года – но об этом мне неизвестно.

Д.»

В добавлении к напечатанной заметке, другой мусульманин написал мне краткое разъяснение в защиту мусульман внутренней России которые, как помнится автору записки, нашли обязательной молитву каждую пятницу в мечети за Его Императорское величество. Вот это разъяснение:

اعوذ بالله من الشيطان الرجيم  و اطيعو الرسول و الوا الامير

«О, будьте вы покорными и верными Богу, Пророку Его, Повелителя вашим и Правительству (**Автор, разъясняя, пытался привести арабский текст Корана (глава 4, статья 62), но почему-то не вписал последних слов «из вас», то есть из мусульман, Он же не указал, где в Шариате говорится об обязательности (для) мусульман молиться за иноверных правителей... Н.О.*).

В книге Шариата сказано, что Шариат повелевает любить родину, которая кормит и быть... (без различия нации и веры), который охраняет. Сее последнее указание Шариата российские улемы толкуют и объясняют <u>различно</u>, и мне <u>помнится</u>, молиться за Русского царя они нашли обязательным, почему в России, в каждой мечети, еженедельно в пятницу после праздничной молитвы (джума) мулла приглашает всех молящихся в мечети, молиться за <u>Его Императорское Величество</u>, тем и оканчивается моление».(5[a])

Печатную заметку корреспондента Д. и рукописное объяснение другого мусульманина я считаю неудовлетворительным, потому что она не устанавливает точного ответа на главный вопрос: кто и когда впервые подал российским и туркестанским мусульманам мысль об обязательности для них молитвы за русского царя, несмотря на его иноверие. Автор печатной заметки Д. говорит, что «эта молитва не была никем сочинена (!), а форма ее оказалась в законе», но он не указывает в <u>каком</u> законе и не поясняет, согласован ли с узаконением в законе формой молитвы текст, составленный ташкентскими кадиями…. Автор присланной мне записки пытался привести в переводе стих Корана (4 глава, 62 статья), но выпустил конечное местоимение «из вас», подлинная форма этого стиха, в русском переводе читается так: «Верующие! Повинуйтесь Богу, повинуйтесь посланнику сему и тем из вас, которые имеют власть». Это означает, что мусульманам было заповедано в Коране повиноваться, кроме Бога и Мохаммеда, и властителям-мусульманам, но без местоимения из вас смысл приведенного изречения меняется в том смысле, что первым мусульманам было заповедано повиноваться вообще властителям, относящихся к их религии. Поэтому-то российские улемы различно толковали и объясняли предписания Шариата о любви к родине и признали обязательным для мусульман молитвы за русского царя. Но это объяснение находится в противоречии с буквальным смыслом изречения Корана, мусульманские публицисты ссылаются на этот текст в доказательство лояльности российских подданных мусульман, как это было в 1898 году, когда генерал-губернатор Духовской производил расследование беспримерного нападения ферганцев на андижанский лагерь. Когда я указал в печатной записке на пропуск в напечатанном в газете Гаспринского упомянутом тексте Корана (4,62) местоимения «из вас», кавказский муфтий написал генералу Духовскому о своем недовольстве по поводу моей записки, ссылаясь на орденский знак первой степени, пожалованный ему Государем за верность службе.

Корреспондент Д., рассказав о том, что молитва за царя, за наследника и за весь царственный(5[6]) дом была впервые произнесена 29 июля 1888 года в мечети Ходжи Ахрара, в присутствии генерал-губернатора Розенбаха и других начальствующих лиц города Ташкента, упомянутых в №33 «Туркестанских Ведомостях» за 1888 год (***Я там же был на этом торжестве и заявляю,* *что написанное в № 33 «Туркестанских Ведомостей» описание этого события носит характер казенного сообщения*) и затем (будто бы ) произносимый каждую пятницу (подразумевается- в ташкентских соборных мечетях). «Может быть», прибавляет корреспондент Д., распоряжение о чтении молитвы за царя в ташкентских мечетях делались и ранее 1888 года, но ему (корреспонденту) об этом не известно… Как старожил Ташкента, я могу сообщить по этому поводу следующее: «Когда к первому Туркестанскому генерал-губернатору Кауфману обратились ташкентские туземцы с просьбой дать им одну пушку для выстрелов в первый день главного мусульманского праздника (идуль-фитр) с целью возвещения об окончании 30 дневного поста в месяц Рамазан, генерал Кауфман ответил, что не может удовлетворить их просьбу, потому что пушки имеют другие назначения, не имеющие ничего общего с религиозным культом туземцев. Туземцы находчиво согласились на свое подданство русскому царю, о благоденствии которого они молятся в мечетях... На это генерал ответил им, что молиться о благоденствии русского государя похвально, потому что его царственные распоряжения направлены на благо его подданных – туркестанских туземцев, пользующихся наступившим в Туркестане(6[a]) внутренним умиротворением, безопасностью и неприкосновенностью религиозного, семейного и общественного быта, что способствует и материальному благосостоянию туземцев. Но – прибавил генерал – если туземцы и не будут молиться за общего нашего государя, то он не принуждает к этому, потому что в России у русского государя есть много миллионов – единоверцев молитвенников…. После этого туземцы не возобновляли своей просьбы о разрешении им стрелять из царских пушек в день главного мусульманского праздника и генерал Кауфман не настаивал на их молитвах за царя в мечетях, предоставляя это их личному усердию. Мой приезд в

Ташкент в конце августа 1877 года совпал с наступлением мусульманского поста, кажется в начале сентября. Я первую неделю бывал у генерала с докладами по учебному ведомству накануне пятницы (в четверг) и никогда не слышал от него, что в пятницу ташкентские мусульмане произносят в мечетях общую молитву за русского государя. Также и во время исполнения должности генералами Колпаковским и Абрамовым и при генерале Черняеве я не слышал об этом. Но в 1888 году при генерале Розенбахе, в первый раз обратился ко мне начальник города Ташкента, полковник Путинцев, с приказанием генерала рассмотреть известный в Казани сборник «Хутбалык», в котором напечатаны пятничные славословия (хутбы), произносимые в татарских мечетях(6[б]) по окончании пятничного молитвословия. В этих хутбах прославляется единобожие и испрашивается благословение Божие пророку Мохаммеду и его семейству, а затем и царствующему государю, упоминается к какому именно государю (падишаху) благословия хутбы относятся, может быть, к турецкому султану или к бывшему золотоордынскому хану, так как это дело было в обычае у хана Узбека. Повод к рассмотрению «Хутбалыка» был необыкновенный: генерал Розенбах задумал отметить приближающийся день именин своей супруги Ольги Ивановны (11 июля 1888 года) двумя торжествами – сразу новым освещением отстроенного военного собора и особым торжеством в туземном городе по случаю передачи туземному населению восстановленной на царские средства соборной (пятничной) мечети Ходжи Ахрара. Соединение этих двух торжеств было задумано широко и идейно – объединить торжество двух религиозных культов, как доказательство веротерпимости русского управления в Туркестане. Для освящения русского собора в Ташкенте из Верного прибыл епископ Неофит, а для передачи туземцам восстановленной мечети было задумано особое торжество с прочтением молитвы за царя и со выставлением в мечети царского портрета. Книжка «Хутбалык» обновлена малиновым бархатом, а в текст хутбы вписаны имена государя и наследника. Но задуманный генерал-губенатором план соединения двух религиозных торжеств в день именин его супруги не состоялся: 11 июля было совершено епископом Неофитом освящение военного собора, а освящение восстановленной мечети в туземном городе было отложено по неизвестному мне соображению, может быть из несправности, в избежании злоязычной болтовни ташкентских шутников.(7[a]) Так называемое «освещение» Ходжи Ахрарской мечети, по неизвестным мне мотивам, было отложено и состоялось 29 июля при обстановке, не особенно торжественной, а в официальном описании этого торжества (№ 33 «Туркестанские Ведомости») была сглажена по казанскому шаблону. И после того генерал Розенбах никогда не вспоминал об неудавшейся попытке соединить два совершенно различных события – одно православно-церковное, а другое только административное и ничего общего с мусульманским культом не имевшего (***Достаточно иметь при этом в виду, что имам Ходжи Ахрарской мечети, представленный ему непривычной роли – читать хутбу за иноверного государя, а заместитель имама, когда читал казанскую хутбу, так потел и так коверкал читая, собственные имена государя и наследника, что даже генерал Розенбах улыбался. До того была непривычна и комична эта сцена, что говорить о других распоряжениях местным русского правительства относительно молитвы за царя, предполагаемых корреспондентом Д. излишне. А последовавшие в 1892 году холерный бунт в Ташкенте и нападение ферганских туземцев на русский лагерь в 1898 году доказывают, что туркестанские туземцы ни мало не солидарны с молитвой за царя и за царское правительство, что согласно с учением Корана глава 4, статья...*). Не справлялся генерал Розенбах и о том, читается ли в пятницы в ташкентских мечетях хутба за русского государя и за царствующий дом России.

Так продолжалось до 1892 года, когда барону Вревскому кто-то напомнил о молитве за русского царя, новый текст которой был неудачно выработан съездом казиев в Ташкенте и одобрен бароном уже в новой редакции, как сказано выше. В этой последней редакции молитва(7[б]) за русского царя и за российский царствующий дом читалась не в мусульманских медрасах и мечетях, а в русско-туземных школах и на умонастроение туземных мусульман влияния не оказывала. Учащиеся в мадрасах муллы не считали себя обязанными запомнить даже только имена царствующей в России фамилии, а «Последнее слово» Багдадского шейха Европе показало, что христианским народам нет оснований надеяться на установление прочных дружественных отношений к мусульманам. Пробужденное революцией 1917 года национальное самосознание мусульман России и Туркестана не удовлетворилось формой союзных республик и побуждало передовых инородцев-мусульман к тайной организации пантюркистских и панисламистских государств, как это известно из сообщений о политическом процессе Касымова в Средней Азии и Султан-Галиева во внутренней России (в Башкирии). На основании изложенных фактов естественно я пришел к заключению, что сама основная идея молитвы за иноверных царей и власти не сродни мусульманам, и была заповедана апостолом Павлом в следующих выражениях:(8[а]) «И так, прежде всего прошу совершить молитвы, прошения, моления, благодарения за всех человеков, за царей и за всех начальствующих, дабы проводить нам жизнь тихую и без мятежную во всяком благочестии и чистоте, ибо это хорошо и угодно Спасителю нашему Богу, который хочет, чтобы все люди спаслись и достигли истины» (Первое послание, глава 2, статья 1-4). Иисус: «Великая душа да будет показана высшим властям: ибо сия власть не от Бога; существующая же власти от Бога установлены. Посему противящийся власти противится Божию установлению; а противящиеся сами навлекут на себя осуждение» (Послание к Римлянам, глава 13, статья 1-2). Это предписание Христа апостолам относительно повиновения властям и молитв за них распространено по всему миру и находит подтверждение у немусульманских народов, когда эти народы вступили в общение с христианами. Для туземцев Средней Азии должен представлять интерес такой факт, что христианский обычай молиться за власти был известен Чингисхану и его потомкам. Академик В. В. Бартольд в своей статье «История турецко-монгольских народов» (Ташкент, 1928 г. страница 16) говорит, что христианство, может быть, при участии уйгуров получило в 13 веке широкое распространение в Монголии. Согласно с этим предположением академика Бартольда, мы находим в сборнике законов Чингисхана «Яса» или «Ясак» определенное указание на обычай молитвы христианским духовенством за царя.(8[б])

В указе Чингисхана, данном на имя главы тибетского религиозного учения в 1223 году говорится: «Светейшее повеление царя Чингиза, повеление начальникам всех мест. Какие есть у Цю-шен-сяня скиты и дома подвижничества, в них ежедневно читающие священные книги и молящиеся небу пусть молятся о долгоденствии царя на многие лета»...

В 1270 году хан Менгу-Темур писал в указе относительно духовенства на Руси: «Все... принадлежит Богу и сами они Божьи. Да помолятся они о нас».

Хан Берке, брат Батыя, отпустил на храм ростовского митрополита Кирилла годовой оброк со всей Ростовской земли за то, что по всему Ростову пели молитвы о здравии ханского сына, который действительно выздоровел.

По молитвам митрополита Московского Алексия, Ханьена ....(Тайдула, жена хана Джанибека, сына Узбек-хана) была исцелена от смерти и за это брала многих русских под свою защиту (***Книга доктора Эленжен Хара-даван «Чингис-хан как полководец и его наследие», Белград,1929 г., стр 213-214*).(9[а])

В «Сборнике материалов, относящихся к истории Золотой Орды», изданном В. Тизенгаузеном в 1884 году в Петербурге, встречаются упоминания о молитве за царствующих мусульманских халифов, султанов, ханов. Так, в хронике секретаря египетского султана Бейбарса, казия Ибн Абдуззахира (умер в 1293 году христианской эры) рассказывается, что султан Бейбарс полюбил Берке, монгольского хана Золотой Орды, и молится о победе его над неприятелями (страница 57) и что в пятницу 7 июня 1263 года (по христианскому летоисчелению) аббасидский халиф Альхаким би-амриллах прочитал молитву за султана Египта и за ордынского хана Берке (страница 58) Египетский султан написал, чтобы за хана Берке молились в Мекке, Медине и Иерусалиме, когда после хан Берке будет в этих священных городах и чтобы в эктении (Хутбе?) поминали Берке после султана (страницы 61-62). В хронике Эль-Муфаддаля упоминается, что во всех владениях хана Узбека (потомка Берке) с амвонов молились молитвой за египетского султана Эль-малика Эн насыра после молитвы за татарского царя Узбека (страница 198). В хронике Ибн-Батуты (умер в 1347 году христианской эры) рассказано, что когда (Ибн-Батута) был в гостях у Азовского Эмира, то после угощения чтец произнес по-арабски красноречивую проповедь об молящихся за Узбека-хана, за Азовского Эмира и за присутствующих (страница 285). Но в опубликованных хрониках арабских путешественников по владениям золотоордынских ханов не упоминается о молитве мусульман за московских князей. (9[б]) И тем более нельзя предположить, чтобы казанские, астраханские и крымские татары после покорения их русскими иноверцами, молятся за своих покорителей потому что они были неверными, а за неверных в Коране молитв не произносилось.

## *Text 3.2:*

## *Khuṭba for the Russian tsar (first version)*

پادشاه اعظم ایمپیراتور حضرتلاری نینك حق لاریغه
اوقولادورغان
خطبه

1. ای بار خدایا پادشاه اعظم ایمپیراتوریمز الیکساندر
الیکساندروویچ غه
واهلیهء محترمه لاری ایمپیراتریتسه معظمه ماریه فیدوروونه غه و
پادشاه
اعظم ایمپیراتور یمز نینك ولی عهد فرزند لاری نیکالای الیکسندروویچ
غه
و بارچه همایون خانه دان عالی لاریغه مهربان بولوب کوب یل لار
اوز
محافظتینك ده ساقلاغیل و اول عالم پناه لارنی صحت سلامت تحت
حمایتینك ده
امان قیلیب و عافیت مندلیك عطا ایلاب اول جناب عالی لاریغه تمامی
ایش لاریده بلند رواج بیرغیل
2. پروردکارا پادشاه اعظم ایمپیراتور یمز نینك پادشاه لیك
عصرینی
مبارك قیلیب اول عالم پناه غه روسسیه مملکتی نینك دشمن لاریغه
غلبه ایلاماق ده و هر خیل بدکارلارغه خوف و هراس سالماق ده
و صالح لارغه مرحمت ایلاماق ده و بیچاره لارغه و بلاغه مبتلا
بولغان لارغه
مدد برماق ده وهم اوزلاریغه تابع تمامی رعیه لارنینك عافیت مندلیك
لاریغه
اتادیك خرسند بولماقده معین بولغیل
3. آلهی پادشاه اعظم ایمپیراتور یمزنینك عصریده بزنینك همه
میزغه
سلامت لیك و خاطرجمع لیك و یخشی هوا و آب فراوان وبرکت
باران

ویرلاریمزدین کوب حاصل بریب دنیا و آخرتیمز نی آباد قیلغیل
آمین یارب العالمین

جناب ترکستان کینیرال کوبیرناتوری بارون وریوسکی نینك
امرلاریغه موافق
ترکستان ولایتی ده غی تمامی مسلمان مسجدلاریده ایام نامه ده ایتیلکان اولوغ
بایرام کون لاریده بول خطبه نی اوقوماق لازم دور پادشاه لیك

## *Text 3.3:*

## *Khuṭba for the Russian tsar (revised version)*

### حق لاریغه پادشاه اعظم ایمپیراتور حضرتلاری نینك اوقولادورغان

### خطبه

1. ای بار خدایا پادشاه اعظم ایمپیراتوریمز نیکالای الیکساندروویچ غه
واهلیهء محترمه لاری کوسودارینه ایمپیراتریتسه معظمه الیکساندرا فیودوروونه غه و هم والده عالم پناه لاری ایمپیراتریتسه معظمه ماریه فیدوروونه
و پادشاه اعظم ایمپیراتور یمز نینك ولیعهد برادرلاری اولوغ کناز ناسلیدنیك کیورکی الیکساندرروویچ غه و برچه همایون خانه دان عالی لاریغه مهربان بولوب کوب یل لار اوزی نینك امان قیلیب و عافیتمندلیك
عطا ایلاب اول شهنشاه لارغه تمامی ایش لاریده بلند رواج بیرغیل
2. پروردکارا پادشاه اعظم ایمپیراتور یمز نینك پادشاه لیك عصرینی
مبارك قیلیب اول عالم پناه غه روسسیه مملکتی نینك دوشمن لاریغه غلبه ا یلاماق ده و هر خیل بدکارلارغه خوف و هراس سالماق ده

و صالح لارغه مرحمت ایلاماق ده و بیچاره لارغه و بلاغه مبتلا بولغان لارغه
مدد برماق ده وهم اوزلاریغه تابع تمامی رعیه لارنینك عافیت مندلیك لاریغه
پدرمقامی دیك خرسند بولماقده معین بولغیل
3. آلهی پادشاه اعظم ایمپیراتور یمزنینك عصریده بزنینك همه میزغه
سلامت لیك و خاطرجمع لیك و یخشی هوا و آب فراوان وبرکت باران
و یرلاریمزدین کوب حاصل بریب دنیا و آخرتیمز نی آباد قیلغیل
آمین یارب العالمین
جناب ترکستان کینیرال کوبیرناتوری بارون وریوسکی نینك
امرلاریغه موافق ترکستان ولایتی ده غی تمامی مسلمان مسجدلاریده
و روسسیه مکتب لاریده اولوغ پادشاه لیك بایرام کون لاریده بول
خطبه نی اوقوماق لازم دور
مذکور اولوغ پادشاه لیك بایرام کون لار 23 اپریل و 4 مای و25
مای 22 ایول و 21 اکتابرده 14 نویابر و 26 نویابر و هم 6 دیکابر دور

## *Text 3.4:*

## *Persian text about a meeting convened in Tashkent by the Russian governor-general (as translated p. 63f., note 188)*

...در تاریخ غره محرم الحرام مطابق سال کوسفند 1300 بودکه شیرنیوف کوبیرناطر برای ترویج شرایع محمدی صلی الله علیه و سلم درون بلده تاشکند در مسجد جامع حضرت خواجه احرار ولی اشرافان و علمایان و فضلایان و اکابران و اعیان و قبایلان را حاضر کردانیده جمهور خلایق عامه غفیر و کثیر و انتخاب علما و فضلا از چهار ارکان بلده اختیار بثلاثه ذو فنان زمان نموده اند اول از رکن حضرت شیخاوندطهوریان زبده دوران جناب متبحر وقت ایشان شریف خواجه قاضی ولد اعز ارشد ایشان پادشاه خواجه زیباچی و ملا ابو القاسم خلیفه و ملا منهاج قاری و از رکن بیش اغاج سجاده نشین زمان ابو القاسم خان ایشان و ایشان عادل خواجه و ملا اعظم قاضی و از رکن کوکچه ملا بایمیرزا آخوند و داملا هادی و اعلم و ملا صالح آخوند خلیفه

و از رکن سیبزاریان ملا عزیز لارخان اعلم و ملا عبد الرسول اعلم و ایشان آرتوق خواجه حاجی خلیفه باین مجموع العلمایانرا اهل بلده تاشکند امور کلی و جزئی شرایع محمدی صلی الله علیه و سلم را تفویض نموده از تعامل عرفیه رسمیه را نیز کذاشته در قباله های اتفاقی نامهارا تحریر نموده بآن صاحب الاختیاران اکابران دوران و الا زمان سپاریده اند دران اذدحام رستخیر و دران معبد خانه متبرکه مشك بیز فقاهت مآب زبده فطانت اکتساب افقه دوران و اعلم الدهر و الاوان و حکمای زمان داملا هادی اعلم عالمان خطاب باین اضعف الطلاب نموده چنین تقریر لسانی کرده اندکه ای شیرازه بند حوادثات پریشانی نکته سنج طغرای واقعات نسب نامه سلسله سلطانی بنتیجه بهبود توامان رونق مروج ادیان اسلامی و اهل اعیانی و ملل محمدی صلی الله علیه وسلم مشتمل بسه علامات متفق و اجتماع ورزید علامات اول انکه امروز ابتدأ هفته است دویم انکه غره ماه محرم و ابتدا نوشتن تاریخ سال است سیوم انکه یکهزارسیصدرا همین روز نوشتیم که روس ثلاثه مائه شد و دیکر ان امور عظیم به ترویج دین احمدی امروز باتمام رسید و خاتمه این امور یوما فیوما و هلم جرا الی آخره در ترقی افزاید و چندین شهور و آسال ماضی و استقبالی باین ذیل و باین مرتبه نتیجه نه بخشیده و تجدد اهل عالم باین نمط متجدد نکردیده و نشنیده که کل جدید لذیذ...

## *Basic abbrevations*

$EI^2$ – Encyclopedia of Islam. New edition. Leiden, London.

DVO – Domusul'manskie verovaniia i obriady. Moskva, 1975.

OIRUz – Institut Vostokovedenia Akademii nauk Respubliki Uzbekistan imeni Abu Raikhana Biruni.

SVR – Sobranie vostochnykh rukopisei v 11 tomakh. Tashkent, 1952-1987.

TVG – Turkistān vilāyatīning gazītī (Turkestanskaia tuzemnaia gazeta).

TsGARUz – Tsentral'nyi Gosudarstvennyi arkhiv Respubliki Uzbekistan.

VOHDSp – Katalog sufischer Handschriften aus der Bibliothek des Instituts für Orientalistik der Akademie der Wissenschaften, Republik Uzbekistan. In: Verzeichnis der Orientalischen Handschriften in Deutschland. Supplementband 37. Hg. J. Paul. Stuttgart, 2002.

# *Bibliography*


Abdurasulov, A. *Khiva (tarikhi-etnografik ocherklar).* Toshkent, 2000.

Abramzon, S. A. *K kharakteristike shamanstva v starom bytu kirgizov.* In: Kratkoe soobshchenia Instituta etnografii. Nr. 30. Moskva, 1958, 149- 159.

Abu-l-Fazl Baikhaki. *Istoria Mas"uda (1030-1041).* Ed. A. K. Arends. 2. Edition. Moskva, 1969.

Akimushkin, S. F. *Opisanie persidskikh i tadzhikskikh rukopisei instituta Vostokovedeniia. Poeticheskie sborniki, al'bomy.* Nr. 10. Moskva, 1993.

Alisher Navoii. *Munozhot.* Ed. S. Ganieva. Toshkent, 1991.

Allworth, E.A.: *The Modern Uzbeks. From the Fourteenth Century to the Present. A Cultural History.* Stanford CA 1990.

*Arabskie rukopisi instituta Vostokovedeniia. Kratkii katalog.* Pod redaktsiei A. B. Khalidova. Part 1. Moskva, 1986.

Ash"or-i nisvon. *Zhomi"` va musakhkhikh I. Davron.*

A"zamov, A. *Munozhotnoma. Alisher Navoiining "Munozhot" asariga sharkhlar.* Toshkent, 2001.

Babadžanov, B., Dūkčī Īšān und der Aufstand von Andižan. – In: *Muslim Culture in Russia and Central Asia from the 18th to the Early 20th Centuries.* Vol. 2: *Inter-Regional and Inter-Ethnic Relations.* Ed. A.v. Kügelgen, M. Kemper, A. Frank. Berlin 1998 (Islamkundliche Untersuchungen : 216), 167-191.

----- *Xalwat-i ṣūfīhā (The Religious Landscape of Khorezm at the Turn of the 19th Century),* with bibliography and index. In: *Muslim Culture in Russia and Central Asia.* Vol. 3: *Arabic, Persian and Turkic Manuscripts (15th-19th Centuries).* Ed. A. v. Kügelgen, A. Muminov, M. Kemper. Berlin 2000 (Islamkundliche Untersuchungen : 233), 113-217.

Baionii Mukhammad Yusuf. *Shazharii Khorazmshokhii*. Ed. N. Dzhumakhuzha, I. Adizova. Toshkent, 1994.
Baldauf I. *Jadidism in Central Asia within Reformism and Modernism in the Muslim World*. In: *Die Welt des Islams*. Band 41,1; 2001, 72-88.
Bartol'd V. V. *Sochineniia*. Vol. 6. Moskva, 1966.
Basilov, V. N. *Kul't sviatykh v islame*. Moskva, 1970.
Bell, R. *The Qur'ān*. Vol. 1-2. Edinburgh, 1937.
Bendrikov, K. E. *Ocherki po istorii narodnogo obrazovaniia v Turkestane (1865-1924)*. Moskva, 1960.
Bertel's, E. E. Sufizm i sufiiskaia literatura. Moskva, 1965.
Bezertinov, R.N. *Tengrianstvo – religiia tiurkov i mongolov*. Naberezhnye Chleny. 2000.
Demidov, S. D. *Magtymy (Istoriko-etnograficheskii etiud)*.In: DVO. 1975.169-190.
*Der Islam. III. Islamische Kultur - Zeitgenössische Strömungen - Volksfrömmigkeit*. Stuttgart, Berlin, Köln, 1990.
Divaev, A. A. *Etnograficheskie materialy. Legendy, byliny, demonologicheskie rasskazy, primety, poslovitsy i skazki tuzemnogo naseleniia Syr-Dar'inskoi oblasti*. Vyp. 1. Tashkent, 1896.
----- *Etnograficheskie materialy. Legendy, byliny, demonologicheskie rasskazy, primety, poslovitsy i skazki tuzemnogo naselenia Syr-Dar`inskoi oblasti*. Vyp. 5. Tashkent, 1898.
----- *Iz oblasti kirgizkikh verovanii. Baksy kak lekar` i koldun (etnograficheskii ocherk)*. Kazan', 1899. 5-34.
----- *Kirgizkie bolezni i sposoby ikh lecheniia*. In: *Turkestanskie vedomosti*, 1902. №80.
Dilshod. *Anbar Otin. She"rlar*. Toshkent, 1994.
*Encylopedia of Islam*. New edition. Leiden: E. J. Brill, 1960-2002.
*Entsiklopediiai adabieti va san"ati tozhik*. Zhild II. Dushanbe, 1989.
Ernazarov, T. E., Akbarov, A. I. *Istoriia pechati Turkestana (1870-1917)*. Tashkent, 1976

Guliamov, Ia. *Pamiatniki goroda Khivy. Trudy Uzbekistanskogo filiala AN SSSR.* Seriia 1. Istoriia, arkheologiia. 1941.
Ibrat, Siddikii Ajzii, Sufizoda. *Tanlangan asarlar.* Ed. B. Kosimov, U. Dolimov, S. Akhmedov. Toshkent, 1999.
*Ipak yuli afsonalari (Zhoi nomlari bilan boglik afsonalar).* Ed. M. Zhuraev. Toshkent, 1993.
*Istoriografiia obshchestvennykh nauk v Uzbekistane.* Ed. Lunin, B. V. Tashkent, 1974.
Iomud khan Karash khan ogli. *Zykyr u Turkmen Zakaspiiskoi oblasti.* In: *Izvestiia Turkestankogo otdela russkogo geograficheskogo obshchestva.* Vol. XVII. Tashkent, 1924, 143-145.
Ivanov, P. P. *Arkhiv khivinskikh khanov XIX v.* Leningrad, 1940.
*Farhang-i fārsī.* Jild 4. Teheran. 1371.
Fasikh Akhmad ibn Dzhalal ad-din Mukhammad al-Khavafi. *Mudjmal-i fasikhi.* Ed. D. Iu. Iusupova. Tashkent, 1980.
Fil'shtinskii, I. M. *Istoriia arabskoi literatury: V- nachalo X veka.* Moskva, 1985.
Firdavs al-iqbāl. *History of Khorezm.* By Shir Muhammad Mirab Munis and Muhammad Riza Mirab Agahi. Translated from Chaghatay and annotated by Y. Bregel. Leiden, Boston, Köln, 1999.
Fozilbek Otabek ugli. *Dukchi Eshon vokeasi. Farghonada istibdod zhallodlari.* S. Akhmad, U. Dolimov, Sh. Risaev nashri. Toshkent, 1992.
*Handlist of Sufi manuscripts ($18^{th}$-$20^{th}$ centuries) in the holdings of the Oriental Institute, Academy of Sciences, Republic of Uzbekistan (Biruni).* Berlin, 2000.
Hutbe. *İslam ansiklopedisi.* 5(1). Istanbul, 1950, 617-620.
Kastan'e, I. *Iz oblasti kirgizskikh verovanii. O charuiushchikh silakh, zakliuchaiushikhsia v cheloveke. Otdel'nyi ottisk iz Vestnika orenburgskogo uchebnogo okruga za 1913 g.* Tashkent, 1913.

KFIR: *Katalog fonda instituta rukopisei.* Vol. 1, Tashkent, 1989.
Khalid, A. *The Politics of Muslim Cultural Reform: Jadidism in Central Asia.* Oxford, 2000.
Khalidov, A. *Khutba.* In: *Islam: Entsiklopedicheskii slovar'.* Moskva, 1991, 285.
*Khorezm: kratkii spravochnik-putivoditel'.* Tashkent, 1962.
Kleinmichel, S. *Ḫalpa in Choresm (Ḫ^w ārazm) und ātin āyi im Ferghanatal: Zur Geschichte des Lesens in Uzbekistan im 20. Jahrhundert* 2 Bde. Berlin, 2000. (Anor 4: 1,2).
Krämer, A. *Geistliche Autorität und islamische Gesellschaft im Wandel. Studien über Frauenälteste (otin and xalfa) im unabhängigen Uzbekistan.* Berlin, 2002.
Kustanaev, Kh. *Etnograficheskie ocherki kirgiz Perovskogo i Kazalinskogo uezdov.* Tashkent, 1894.
*Le livre de Babur: Babur-nama. Mémories du premier Grand Mogol des Indes (1494-1529). Présenté et traduit du turc tchaghatay par J. L. Bacqué-Grammont.* Paris, 1985.
*Leonid Pavlovich Potapovs Materialien zur Kulturgeschichte der Usbeken aus den Jahren 1928-1930.* Hg. J. Taube. Wiesbaden, 1995.
----- *Lion of Tashkent: The Career of General M. G. Cherniaev.* Athens, Ga.,1974.
Lunin, B. V. *Iz istorii russkogo vostokovedeniia i arkheologii v Turkestane. Turkestanskii kruzhok liubitelei arkheologii: (1895-1917).* Tashkent, 1958.
MacKenzie, D. *Kaufman of Turkestan: An Assessment of His Administration (1867-1881).* In: *Slavic Review*; No. 26. 1967, 265-285.
Makhmud ibn Vali. *More tain otnositel'no doblestei blagodarnykh (geografiia).* Ed. B. A. Akhmedov. Tashkent, 1977.
Malov, S. E. *Ostatki shamanstva u zheltykh uigurov. In: Zhivaia starina. Otdelenie etnografii russkogo geograficheskogo obshchestva.* Nr. 1. Sankt-Peterburg, 1912, 61-70.
Miropiev, M. *Demonologicheskie rasskazy kirgizov.* In: *Zapiski imperatorskogo rossiiskogo geograficheskogo*

*obshchestva po otdelu etnografii.* Vol. V nr. 3, Sankt-Peterburg, 1888, 61-70.

*Munājātnāma-i Khᵛāja ʿAbdallāh Anṣārī va rubāʿīyāt.* Tihrān, 1376.

Munirov, K. *Khorazmda tarikhnavislik.* Toshkent, 2002.

*Munozhot.* In: *Uzbek sovet entsiklopediasi.* Vol. 7. Toshkent, 1976, 424.

Murodov, O. *Shamanskii obriadovoi fol'klor u tadzhikov srednei chasti doliny Zeravshan.* In: DOV, 1975, 94-122.

*Opisanie Khivinskogo pokhoda 1873.* Ed. V. N. Trotskii. Sankt-Peterburg, 1898.

Ostroumov, N. *Pervyi opyt slovaria narodno-tatarskogo iazyka po vygovoru kreshchennykh tatar Kazan'skoi gubernii.* Kazan', 1876.

----- *Mukhammedanskii post v mesiats ramazan.* Kazan', 1877.

----- *Chto takoe Koran?* Tashkent, 1883.

----- *Istoria teksta Korana.* Tashkent, 1900.

----- *Koran i progress.* Ed. A. L. Kirsner. Tashkent, 1901.

----- *Sarty.* Vyp. 3. Tashkent, 1895.

----- *Sarty.* 2. Edition. Tashkent, 1896.

----- *Sarty.* 3. Edition, continued. Tashkent, 1908.

----- *Etimologiia sartovskogo iazyka.* Tashkent, 1910.

----- *Islamovedenie.* 1. edition, 1910; 2. edition, 1912; 3. edition, 1914. Tashkent.

----- *Sovremennoe pravovoe polozhenie musul'manskoi zhenshchiny.* Kazan', 1911.

----- *Araviia i Koran (proiskhozhdenie i kharakter islama). Opyt istoricheskogo issledovania.* Kazan', 1899.

----- *Materialy k izucheniiu narechiia sartov russkogo Turkestana. Stikhi v chest' ramazan (sartskii tekst i russkii perevod).* Kazan', 1899.

----- *O musul'manskikh tainikh pismenakh „kamsaliatabgiz".* In: *Protokol zasedaniia i soobshchenia chlenov Turkestan-skogo kruzhka liubitelei archelogii.* 21. god. Tashkent, 1917, 71-86.

----- *Perevod iarlyka Kokandskogo khana.* In: *Protokol zasedaniia i soobshcheniia chlenov Turkestanskogo kruzhka liubitelei arkheologii.* 21. god. Tashkent, 1917, 24-26.

*Pakhlavon Makhmud (Khazrati Pakhlavon ota khikoiatlari).* Toshkent, 2001.

Rakhmonov, A., Yusipov, S. *Khorazmda "mukaddas zhoilar" va ularning vuzhudiga kelish sirlari.* Toshkent, 1963.

Rtveladze, L., Rtveladze, E. *Musul'manskie sviatyni Uzbekistana.* Tashkent, 1996.

Rzehak, L. *Vom Persischen zum Tadschikischen: Sprachliches Handeln und Sprachplanung in Transoxanien zwischen Tradition, Moderne und Sowjetmacht (1900-1956).* Wiesbaden, 2001.

Samoilovich, A. *Dva otryvka iz „Khorezm-name".* In: *Zapiski Vostochnogo otdeleniia Imperatorskogo Russkogo Arkheologicheskogo Obshchestva.* Vol. XIX. Sankt-Peterburg, 1909, 78-83.

SVR, vol. II, 1954; vol. IV, 1957; vol. V, 1960; vol. VII, 1964, Tashkent.

Semenov, A. *Pokoritel' i ustroitel' Turkestanskogo kraia general-adiudant K. P. fon-Kaufman.* In: *Kaufmanskii sbornik izdannyi v pamiat' 25 let, istekshikh so dnia smerti pokoritelia i ustroitelia Turkestanskogo kraia general-adiudanta K. P. fon-Kaufman 1st.* Moskva, 1910.

Shikhab ad-din Mukhammad an-Nasavii. *Zhizneopisanie Sultana Dzhalal ad-dina Mankburny.* Ed. Z. M. Buniatov. Baku, 1973.

Sidkii Khondailikii. *Tanlangan asarlar.* Ed. B. Kasimov, R. Dzhabkharova. Toshkent, 1998.

Siscoe, F., Schuyler, E. *General Kaufman and Central Asia.* In: *Slavic Review*; No. 1, 1968, 119-124.

Snesarev, G. P. *Relikty domusul'manskikh verovanii i obriadov u uzbekov Khorezma.* Moskva, 1969.

----- *Khorezmskie legendy kak istochnik po istorii religioznykh kul'tov Srednei Azii.* Moskva, 1983.

*Spisok pechatnykh trudov direktora Turkestanskoi uchitel'skoi seminarii N. P. Ostroumova za vremia sluzhby ego v Turkestanskom krae s 1877 po 1917 gody*. Sasove, 1920.
*Sufizm v Tsentral'noi Azii (zarubezhnye issledovaniia). Sbornik statei pamiati Fritsa Maiera (1812-1998)*. Ed. A. A. Khismatullin. Sankt-Peterburg, 2001.
Sukhareva, O. A. *K voprosu o kul'te musul'manskikh sviatykh v Srednei Azii.* In: *Trudy instituta istorii i arkheologii Uz AN. T. II*, 47-63, 1951.
----- *Perezhitki demonologii i shamanstva u ravninykh tadzhikov*. In: DOV, 1975, 5-93.
Tavaslı, Y. *Musulman Ailenin izahlı tam dua kitabı*. İstanbul. 1990.
*The Holy Bible. Revised Standard Version*. 2. Edition. Glasgow, New York, Toronto, 1971.
Tizengauzen, V. *Sbornik materialov, otnosiashchikhsia k istorii Zolotoi Ordy*. Sankt-Peterburg, 1884.
Tolstova, L. S. *Istoricheskie predaniia iuzhnogo priaralia: k istorii rannykh etnokul'turnykh sviazei Aralo-kaspiiskogo regiona*. Moskva, 1984.
Tukhtametov, T. G. *Rossiia i Khiva v kontse XIX –nachala XX vv. Pobeda Khorezmskoi narodnoi revoliutsii*. Moskva, 1969.
*Uzbekistonning yangi tarikhi: birinchi kitob. Turkiston chor Rossiasi mustamlakachiligi davrida*. Toshkent, 2000.
Zhalolov, A., Uzganboev, Kh. *Uzbek ma"rifatparvarlik adabietining tarakkietida vaktli matbuotning urni ("Turkiston viloiatining gazeti", "Tarakkii", "Samarkand", "Sadoi Turkiston" kunnomalari asosida)*. Toshkent, 1993.

Bei Fragen zur Produktsicherheit wenden Sie sich bitte an:
If you have any questions regarding product safety,
please contact:

Walter de Gruyter GmbH
Genthiner Straße 13
10785 Berlin
productsafety@degruyterbrill.com